Early Praise for *Modern CSS with Tailwind: Flexible Styling Without the Fuss*

This book is a great introduction to the Tailwind utility CSS framework. Having used Tailwind on a project for the first time after reading the book, it helped to prime knowledge I needed to use Tailwind successfully and also served as a valuable reference guide.

➤ **Kevin Murphy**
   Software Developer

I think this book is a wonderful resource and will give many readers the insight they need to be proficient with Tailwind CSS.

➤ **John Saltarelli**
   Chief Technology Officer, Unit 5 Ventures, Inc.

This book helped my team and me migrate our project with hundreds of templates to Tailwind. It covers all the important topics, encourages a useful mindset when working with the framework, and includes many great little tips along the way.

➤ **Matouš Borák**
   Chief Technology Officer, NejRemeslnici.cz

Modern CSS with Tailwind, Second Edition

Flexible Styling Without the Fuss

Noel Rappin

The Pragmatic Bookshelf

Raleigh, North Carolina

For our complete catalog of hands-on, practical, and Pragmatic content for software developers, please visit *https://pragprog.com*.

The team that produced this book includes:

CEO: Dave Rankin
COO: Janet Furlow
Managing Editor: Tammy Coron
Development Editor: Katharine Dvorak
Copy Editor: L. Sakhi MacMillan
Layout: Gilson Graphics
Founders: Andy Hunt and Dave Thomas

For sales, volume licensing, and support, please contact *support@pragprog.com*.

For international rights, please contact *rights@pragprog.com*.

ISBN-13: 978-1-68050-940-3
Book version: P1.0—May 2022

Contents

Acknowledgments

This book was a surprise. I didn't intend to write it, but I got excited about the subject and had an unusual window of time to get this done.

Thanks to Katharine Dvorak, who edited this book and has now edited several of my books. Katie was very supportive of this from my initial suggestion. We've been working together for years now, and her observations have been a tremendous help in structuring and planning this book.

Dave Rankin at The Pragmatic Bookshelf was enthusiastic about this book when I first suggested it, and then he was flexible in approach when the original plan for the book's structure didn't seem like the best way to present the material.

Thanks to Adam Wathan for creating Tailwind and to all the people who have contributed to its development.

Gary Bernhardt and Dave Copeland both in different ways helped me see the value in utility-based CSS, and Aly Fluckey showed me that CSS could be beautiful.

The first edition of this book was reviewed by Erik Benoist, Matouš Borák, Kevin Murphy, John Saltarelli, and Jonathan Yeong, and the second edition was again reviewed by Matouš Borák, Kevin Murphy, and John Saltarelli. The book is better because of their input and advice.

Thanks always to my family. Amit and Elliot continue to be amazing and delightful. Erin makes everything I do easier, better, and more fun.

Preface to the Second Edition

This book covers Tailwind 3.0, which significantly changes the way Tailwind CSS works and the way most developers will interact with it.

Tailwind 3.0 adds a *just-in-time* (JIT) engine, which changes the way Tailwind determines what Cascading Style Sheets (CSS) code to generate and make available to the browser. Tailwind is a large set of CSS classes that each stand in for some set of CSS properties. In previous versions, Tailwind generated a list of its CSS classes and then allowed you to specify any classes in that list you wanted removed to limit the size of the Tailwind file for performance purposes.

The JIT engine reverses that process. The Tailwind command-line tool now starts with an empty file and adds utility CSS classes to that file based on patterns it matches with your front-end code. By no longer needing to be able to pre-enumerate all the possible Tailwind classes, the tool is freed up to be far more flexible and powerful. For example, Tailwind now allows you to specify the background color and opacity in one class, as in bg-yellow-700/50, with the color listed first and the opacity after the slash. Previously, the number of potential classes that syntax would allow would have made managing it prohibitively expensive.

Tailwind provides a series of modifiers that conditionally apply classes under certain conditions, such as hover or focus. In previous versions of Tailwind, only a small subset of the modifiers were enabled by default because each added its own entire Tailwind-sized set of potential classes. With the JIT engine, and no longer needing to start from a list of potential classes, all the modifiers are enabled by default, and several new ones have been added.

In Tailwind 3.0, many features that previously had only a set amount of potential values allow you to use arbitrary values, as in m-[43px] for a margin of exactly 43 pixels. It's not recommended to do that very often—one advantage of Tailwind is the consistency of measurements. Sometimes, though, you need a one-off value, and Tailwind 3.0 makes doing so much easier.

Because of the JIT engine, it's true both that almost all the features you used in Tailwind 2.0 are still here and that they've all gotten a lot more flexible. I've tried to navigate that in this text, to note the additional ability to use arbitrary values in many patterns without endorsing the continual use of those patterns.

In addition, the installation instructions for Tailwind have changed, and there's a new option to use a stand-alone command-line tool that doesn't require NodeJS to be used. Because of that, I've been able to make the sample code for this book much simpler—now it's just a static HTML file and an associated Tailwind CSS file. There have also been some significant changes to specific Tailwind features such as color, and the configuration options have changed somewhat.

So welcome to Tailwind 3.0! If this is your first experience, I hope this book helps you navigate the complexities of the tool. If you were with me for the first edition, I hope you find in this edition a clear guide to the newest version of Tailwind.

Noel Rappin
May 2022

Introduction

Many web developers underrate CSS.

Cascading Style Sheets (CSS) enable you to control the display of your information and enhance your page with visual effects. CSS is powerful, as a quick glance at a site like http://www.csszengarden.com shows. With CSS, you can do amazing things to the basic text and images on your site, and with a little bit of client-side code to add and remove CSS classes, you can do exponentially more.

CSS can also be hard to debug, complicated to write, and difficult to control.

But it doesn't have to be.

Enter Tailwind. Tailwind CSS—a "utility-first" CSS framework to "rapidly build modern websites without ever leaving your HTML"[1]—can make the CSS for your site easier to control and debug. In this book, you'll dive into the Tailwind CSS framework, taking a look at its typography, page layout, responsive design, and more.

Why Tailwind?

Bootstrap or similar CSS frameworks provide CSS classes whose names describe the semantics how they are to be used, like "button" or "card" or "nav." These classes tend to define a number of CSS styles together.

Tailwind is different.

Nearly all of the basic Tailwind utility classes are thin wrappers around a single CSS style setting, like using m-4 to provide a margin: 1rem or text-lg to change the text size to font-size: 1.125rem.

For example, a button in the Bulma framework can be styled like this:

```
<button class="button is-primary">Click Me</button>
```

---

1. https://tailwindcss.com

But in Tailwind, you might use something more like this:

```
<button
  class="bg-green-500 text-white font-bold
         py-3 px-4 rounded-lg text-center">
  Click Me
</button>
```

In the Tailwind version, each individual style of the button—the green background, the white text, the bold font, the padding, the rounded corners, and the text centering—gets its own class in the class list.

Now, if you're like me, your first reaction to seeing that list of classes may be something along the lines of, and I quote, "ugh." It certainly takes some time to get used to having all those small class names in the HTML markup. If that's your reaction, I get it. All I ask is that you give it a chance and see how you feel after you've tried it out.

The Tailwind code is extremely explicit and makes it possible to understand the display simply by looking at the HTML markup. It works well with front-end frameworks that have an aesthetic of putting a bunch of CSS or JavaScript data in the HTML markup. If you want to package a collection of classes for reuse, Tailwind provides an @apply directive that you can use to build new CSS classes out of Tailwind's utilities, but it's recommended that you use features of your web programming language and framework to manage the duplication.

One advantage of the Tailwind setup is that it's extremely easy to prototype, iterate, and customize the display. If you want to change the horizontal padding on a button, you can do so by changing px-4 to, say, px-6. You don't need to guess about the scope of the change or what other parts of your page might be affected. You can keep making small changes until you get the display just right. And you don't need to continually come up with names for CSS property combinations that might not be reused.

Another advantage is that Tailwind offers a set of modifiers that allow you to specify behavior in particular cases. For example, you could add a class such as hover:bg-blue-500, where the hover modifier causes the background color to be changed only when the user hovers over the button. Tailwind also provides a set of modifiers that allow you to specify different behaviors at different screen sizes. These modifiers are one reason why using a Tailwind class like bg-blue-500 is better than using the document object model (DOM) style attribute directly, as in style="background-color: #cdcdcd".

And last but not least, a Tailwind app requires less CSS to be written, with most of the design coming from the composition of Tailwind utilities. This means you spend less time naming CSS and managing global CSS, allowing you to spend more effort on the actual display of your site. Tailwind makes it easy to make incremental changes, see the results, and understand the scope of your changes, which makes it especially useful when prototyping a new site.

About This Book

In this book, you're going to look at how to design web pages using Tailwind CSS version 3.0 and up. You'll start with the typography of individual elements, and then you'll get to "the box"—the rectangle of space each element takes up—and how to manipulate it. Once you have your elements in boxes, you'll take a look at page layout with flexbox or grids.

After that, you'll look at turning individual pages into full sites. You'll also look at common site-wide page layouts, managing a design on different screen sizes, and handling a site-wide amount of styles and CSS.

Tailwind has been evolving pretty quickly, so there's a good chance new features have been added since I wrote this. The Tailwind documentation includes pages for release notes and upgrade guides. (Sorry, the release notes' URLs change with each release, but they're linked from the main Tailwind documentation at https://tailwindcss.com/docs.) Check those out for the latest changes.

Who This Book Is For

To keep this book short and to the point, I've made some assumptions:

- I'm assuming you already know the basics of CSS syntax and concepts. This book focuses on Tailwind, not raw CSS. If you want to get better grounded in CSS and its quirks, you might want to try the zine *Hell Yes! CSS!* by Julia Evans.[2]

- I'm assuming you're able to access the Tailwind reference documentation.[3] The Tailwind documentation is comprehensive and easy to navigate. This book isn't going to be a complete reference on all of Tailwind's features; instead, it'll focus on the most common ones and how to use them successfully.

---

2. https://wizardzines.com/zines/css
3. https://tailwindcss.com/docs

Running the Sample App

The sample code for this book is extremely simple. It consists of a few pages of static HTML linked to a static CSS page that was generated using the Tailwind CLI without using any framework or dynamic content.

To run the sample code, you need to download it from the book's page on the Pragmatic Bookshelf website.[4] To view the code samples, just open any of the HTML pages in the html directory in a browser as a file. They will link to the css/output.css file, which has been pre-generated using the Tailwind CLI. (For more information about using the Tailwind CLI with that code, jump ahead to Using the Sample Code, on page 2.)

Please note that the world has possibly changed since this book was released, and the distribution setup and commands for the Tailwind CLI has changed. If these instructions don't work for you, please check out the book forum[5] for more discussion and support. Thanks!

---

4. https://www.pragprog.com/titles/tailwind2
5. https://devtalk.com/books/modern-css-with-tailwind-second-edition/errata

CHAPTER 1

Getting Started with Tailwind

Before going deep into Tailwind's utilities, let's take a quick tour to get a feel for how Tailwind CSS works.

Tailwind is both a set of utility classes and a tool that generates CSS files based on those classes. It also provides the @apply directive to allow you to compose Tailwind classes. To get started with Tailwind, we need to install the framework itself and then patch it into our CSS processing tool chain. First, we'll take a look at what the Tailwind command-line interface (CLI) does.

What the Tailwind CLI Does

Tailwind, as a set of utility classes, provides a wide variety of patterns that you can use to assign CSS classes to HTML elements in your code.

When you use Tailwind, you write CSS classes whose names match the patterns Tailwind defines. For example, you write <div class="m-4"> and Tailwind defines that in CSS as .m-4 {margin: 1rem;}. Tailwind has the potential to define millions of different CSS classes given that the patterns are both extensive and can be combined with different modifiers, and can even in many cases use arbitrary values. In fact, it's not feasible to enumerate all the potential classes Tailwind might define or use, and your project is likely to only use a small fraction of those classes.

Defining all these potential classes—the vast majority of them unused—and then sending them to the browser would be a huge performance problem. To avoid that problem, Tailwind uses a just-in-time engine to detect the CSS you are using and limit the amount of CSS that is defined, generating only the CSS your project uses. A command-line interface (CLI) to that engine is provided, and your front-end build tool can use that CLI to generate the CSS needed for your project.

You provide Tailwind with a list of the files in your project that declare CSS classes, Tailwind scans those files for text patterns that match Tailwind classes and then creates a CSS file that only contains the Tailwind classes that are actually used.

The Tailwind command line is set up to run fast and err on the side of including extra classes rather than try and guess whether the usage of, say, m-4 is actually part of a CSS declaration. If the text m-4 is in the file anywhere, Tailwind will add m-4 to the resulting CSS.

This is fine because Tailwind patterns are odd enough to only rarely occur accidentally and because including the odd extra CSS class is a small price to pay for excluding millions of others while still including the Tailwind classes you are actually using.

Using the Sample Code

This book has a small amount of sample code associated with it. It's delivered as a set of static HTML files that read a static CSS file. The CSS file was generated using the Tailwind CLI, and you can install that CLI locally if you want to experiment.

You can experiment with the sample code as is using the stand-alone version of the Tailwind CLI, which doesn't require Node.js to run. This may not be the mechanism you use on a full front-end app, so take a look at the next section as well.

To get started with the stand-alone Tailwind CLI, download the latest release for your operating system at https://github.com/tailwindlabs/tailwindcss/releases and place the file at the top level of book's code directory, adjacent to the tailwind.config.js file.

You might want to rename that download to just tailwindcss. For me, that command was mv tailwindcss-macos-arm64 tailwindcss. Your command will vary based on what file you downloaded. You'll also need to make the file executable with something like chmod +x tailwindcss; again your operating system might vary.

With the stand-alone CLI in place, you can tinker with the existing code or add new HTML files in the html directory. Then, when you run the CLI with ./tailwindcss -o css/output.css, it will re-parse the HTML files and regenerate the css/output.css file. Don't worry, we'll talk about everything that command is doing later in the book.

Please note that it's possible that the distribution setup and commands for the Tailwind CLI have changed since the book was written. If these instructions don't work for you, please check out the book forum[1] for guidance.

Adding Tailwind to Your App

The process of installing Tailwind to a front-end app depends on how your project is managing client-side assets. As such, a complete guide to installing Tailwind is outside the scope of this book and would quickly become outdated. The golden source is the Tailwind documentation itself.[2] Please check there if you have difficulty installing Tailwind in your specific setup. This section gives a general overview of how Tailwind is installed for most projects.

The Tailwind developers recommend that the easiest way to install Tailwind for most projects is via the Node.js version of the Tailwind command-line tool. Start by installing Tailwind itself:

```
$ npm install -D tailwindcss
```

Next, run the following command to create a Tailwind configuration file:

```
$ npx tailwind init
```

This creates the following empty configuration file:

```
tailwind.config.js
module.exports = {
  content: ["./html/*.html"],
  theme: {
    extend: {},
  },
  plugins: [],
};
```

You need to add one piece of information to the configuration file for the Tailwind CLI to work. You need to tell Tailwind all the files that might use a CSS class. The Tailwind CLI uses this information as input to the CSS generation process we talked about at the beginning of the chapter.

The information goes in the content property of the configuration and uses standard file matching syntax, where * matches any text, and ** matches any and all subdirectories.

A standard React app might look like this, where Tailwind is directed to look at all files in any subdirectory under src that end in html, js, or jsx:

---

1. https://devtalk.com/books/modern-css-with-tailwind-second-edition/errata
2. https://tailwindcss.com/docs/installation

```
module.exports = {
  content: ["./src/**/*.{html,js,jsx}"],
  theme: {
    extend: {},
  },
  plugins: [],
}
```

A basic Ruby on Rails setup might look like this, matching all view files with html.erb, all helper files with .rb, and all JavaScript files with .js:

```
module.exports = {
  content: [
    './app/views/**/*.html.erb',
    './app/helpers/**/*.rb',
    './app/javascript/**/*.js'
  ],
  theme: {
    extend: {},
  },
  plugins: [],
}
```

Your application will likely have some slightly different setup, but the goal is to have all files that might have CSS information passed to the Tailwind CLI.

If you're using Visual Studio Code, the Tailwind extension uses the existence of the configuration file to determine if the project uses Tailwind. Other integrated development environments (IDEs) and editors also have various plugins and other forms of Tailwind support.

Finally, we need to add Tailwind to our CSS files. In general, you put the following lines in a CSS file that's being imported. The exact location of the file depends on your tooling, but we want it to look like this:

```
css/input.css
@tailwind "tailwindcss/base";
@tailwind "tailwindcss/components";
@tailwind "tailwindcss/utilities";
```

Here we're importing Tailwind in three layers. The base contains Tailwind's reset classes, components is a small layer containing Tailwind's component class, and most of what I'll be talking about in this book is in the utilities layer. The layers become important as you customize Tailwind—if you want to compose your classes with Tailwind modifiers, the classes need to be defined before the utilities layer.

Other build systems might require you to use @import instead of @tailwind as the command; check the official docs as a final source.

That should get you started. Let's now see what Tailwind can do.

Quick Start

We'll quickly run through styling a hero segment for a sample page for a concert series called NorthBy. The sample page in the code shows all the versions one after the other. This is only a page in the public HTML of our server app, so there's no server-side information needed to explain this. (If you're running the sample code, the page should be visible by opening the intro.html page in a browser.)

Here's our first version:

html/intro.html
```
<h1>Welcome to NorthBy</h1>
```

Welcome to NorthBy

You should see no styling applied to the text at all, not even the normal size and bold styling you'd usually associate with an HTML h1 tag. This is a good test of whether Tailwind is installed. If you see any styling applied to the text, then Tailwind isn't loading and you should walk through the installation steps again.

Let's go back and forth between the code and the view to start adding features here with Tailwind. I'm not going to explore the syntax or other options in depth. All I want is to give a sense of what it's like to work with Tailwind as best as I can in a book format.

And, I have to add up front that I'm not a designer.

Here's a first pass at getting a basic layout with text, subtext, and a logo:

html/intro.html
```
<div class="flex">
  <div>
    <img src="../media/music.svg" size="100x100" />
  </div>
  <div>
    <h1>Welcome to NorthBy</h1>
    <h2>A premium in sight and sound</h2>
    <button>Learn More</button>
  </div>
</div>
```

This code gives us the following result:

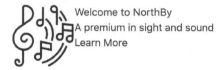

This isn't too different from our first version. There's still no styling applied to the text, and there's no spacing or anything.

Let's add more changes. We can center the text, put a little bit of distance between the two parts, vertically center the text against the logo, and put the logo on the right. The Tailwind classes I'm using do a pretty good job of representing my intent:

```
html/intro.html
<div class="flex justify-center">
  <div class="mx-4 order-last">
    <img src="../media/music.svg" size="100x100" />
  </div>
  <div class="mx-4 self-center">
    <h1>Welcome to NorthBy</h1>
    <h2>A premium in sight and sound</h2>
    <button>Learn More</button>
  </div>
</div>
```

We've added classes here. The outer div now has two Tailwind classes: flex justify-center. The image has another two classes, mx-4 order-last, and the text block also has mx-4 self-center. The mx-4 classes specify horizontal margin, while the rest of the classes all deal with layout using the CSS flexbox structure, which we'll look at later in Flexbox, on page 50.

Now, let's go after that text. Let's make the header big, the subhead less big, and all the lines centered. And let's give the whole thing a background:

```
html/intro.html
<div class="flex justify-center bg-gray-300">
  <div class="mx-4 order-last">
    <img src="../media/music.svg" size="100x100" />
  </div>
  <div class="mx-4 self-center text-center">
    <h1 class="text-6xl font-bold text-blue-700">Welcome to NorthBy</h1>
    <h2 class="text-3xl font-semibold text-blue-300">
      A premium in sight and sound
    </h2>
    <button>Learn More</button>
  </div>
</div>
```

This adds a new class to the outer div, bg-gray-300, which specifies a background color. We've added a bunch of classes to the text elements, including a text-center class surrounding them. The title element is now marked with text-6xl font-bold text-blue-700, which specifies text size, font weight, and color. The sub-head is smaller, less bold, and a lighter shade of blue: text-3xl font-semibold text-blue-300.

Next, let's make the button look more like a button, realign the image, and while we're at it, make the image rounder, too:

```
html/intro.html
<div class="flex justify-center bg-gray-300">
  <div class="mx-4 order-last self-center">
    <img src="../media/music.svg" size="100x100" class="rounded-full" />
  </div>
  <div class="mx-4 self-center text-center">
    <h1 class="text-6xl font-bold text-blue-700">Welcome to NorthBy</h1>
    <h2 class="text-3xl font-semibold text-blue-300">
      A premium in sight and sound
    </h2>
    <button
      class="my-4 px-4 py-2 border-2 border-black rounded-lg
             text-white bg-blue-900 ">
      Learn More
    </button>
  </div>
</div>
```

The image tag now has a class of rounded-full, which makes the whole thing appear in a circle (admittedly quite a subtle effect on this image). The button has grown a lot of classes: my-4 px-4 py-2 specifies a vertical margin and horizontal and vertical padding; border-2 border-black rounded-lg specifies the size, color, and shape of the border; and text-white bg-blue-900 gives us the text and background colors:

Not too bad to start. In each step we were able to incrementally change the display of the code by adding more Tailwind classes to the markup, ending up with a pretty elaborate, if still not finished, design.

And that's only the beginning. We can make this logo look better on smaller screens, we can make the background a gradient (or we can make the text color a gradient), and on and on.

A key point here that's hard to get across in print: this is fun. It's easy to make the incremental changes, see the results, and understand the scope of your changes. Yes, you're seeing snapshots of a process, but the process didn't involve us putting a Tailwind class in and being surprised that it affected something on the page we weren't expecting.

Now, let's look at how Tailwind works and start with some of the basics.

CHAPTER 2

Tailwind Basics

Tailwind seems like a counterintuitive solution to the problem of managing CSS for a complex site. Tailwind is made up of many, many small utility CSS class names, most of which set one specific CSS property to one specific value. The preferred way to get complex behavior in Tailwind is to compose multiple CSS classes together on the HTML element.

This pattern goes against a lot of the CSS naming conventions that have developed over the years. Many CSS frameworks and naming conventions suggest using names that reflect the semantic meaning of the element on the page—names like button, nav-bar, or menu-item.

Tailwind classes aren't semantic at all. They're utility classes, meaning a Tailwind class represents a specific CSS property like font-bold for text formatting or m-6 for margin. Other CSS frameworks include utility classes but consider the semantic class names more important. Using Tailwind and utility classes suggests the potential for a lot of duplication, as Tailwind utility classes are often repeated on multiple DOM elements.

Despite the potential duplication, Tailwind can work on larger sites.

One reason is that when you apply a Tailwind class at any particular point, both the nature of the styling change and the scope of that change are exceptionally clear. Tailwind's short names may seem cryptic at first, but the naming patterns are consistent and become easier to read. Also, Tailwind modifiers make it easy to define special behavior in the HTML, such as hover and responsive behaviors on differently sized screens. The modifiers also make the entirety of an element's styling clearer just by looking at the HTML.

Because you can combine Tailwind classes in arbitrary ways, you write far less external CSS code in Tailwind than you might in another CSS style. You don't need to name as many custom CSS classes when using Tailwind. And because the Tailwind changes are so closely tied to the HTML markup, it's easier to predict the result of making a change.

With Tailwind you can extract a common CSS class from a list of Tailwind utilities and give it a more semantic name. Rather than create your own classes this way, Tailwind recommends taking advantage of the same tools you use in your front-end stack to reduce duplication. For example, rather than creating a separate CSS class for button styles, Tailwind suggests you create a reusable React component or a Rails partial or helper method and define the CSS styles only once for that reusable item.

Tailwind is made up of a few different pieces: the utility classes that we'll spend the bulk of our time working with in this book, a reset style sheet, and functions that make working with Tailwind easier.

Utilities

Tailwind's utility classes are the most important part of Tailwind to understand. Here's how they work and how I'll talk about them in the book.

Tailwind is made up of thousands if not millions of utility classes, most of which set the value of a single CSS property. For example, the font-bold Tailwind utility class is an alias for the CSS property, font-weight: 700. You'd use that utility in an HTML element as part of the class attribute, as in class="font-bold".

There are far, far more potential Tailwind utility classes than you'd ever use in a single project, or that you'd want to send to your browser. To limit the CSS generated, Tailwind has a command-line tool that generates the set of utility CSS classes that are used based on your code. Additionally, the Tailwind configuration file gives you more control over the patterns and names Tailwind looks for. Unless I clearly say otherwise, in this book I'll talk about the default set of classes used by a minimal configuration, and in Chapter 8, Customizing Tailwind, on page 67, I'll talk about how to adjust the names you look for.

Tailwind utilities often come in families with a common pattern of beginnings or endings. When I talk about those, I'll use syntax like this: .text-{size}, to indicate a family of utilities that include .text-xs, .text-sm, .text-xl, and so on. When this syntax is used, the dash is only needed if the part in braces is not empty, so you'll use text-sm but also potentially just text.

The variable part of the utility name doesn't have to be at the end of the name. For example, in margin sizing utilities, .m{direction}-{size} indicates a family of utilities such as .m-0 or .mt-10. As you'll see, the variable part of utilities is often consistent across different parts of Tailwind. For example, the options for {size} and {direction} in the margin utilities are shared by the padding utilities and several other utility families.

Although Tailwind provides a set of defaults for things like sizing and color, you can also use arbitrary values by enclosing them in square brackets. For example, if you have a one-off margin, you could use m-[104px] to indicate a 104 pixel margin, which is not one of the default sizes provided. In general, any place you see a variable placeholder, you can use square brackets to insert an arbitrary value. The use of these arbitrary values is meant for one-off fixes. If you're using the same arbitrary value over and over, you might want to add that value to the configuration file to make it available generally and keep the design consistent.

You can even use square brackets to insert an entire CSS style property if you need to use one that Tailwind doesn't support, like [mask-type:alpha].

Preflight

When you install Tailwind, you need to import three different files with the commands: @tailwind base, @tailwind components, and @tailwind utilities. Each of these files contains a different set of CSS rules. (In some installations, you use the more generic file import command @import rather than @tailwind.)

@tailwind base contains Tailwind's reset style sheet called *Preflight*. A reset style sheet is a restyling of all the base HTML elements to a minimal set of styling properties. Without a reset style sheet, each browser defines its own default set of style properties for how to render individual HTML elements that don't have further CSS properties. Using a reset style sheet gives our application control over this baseline, eliminating differences between browsers and providing a more minimal backdrop into which we insert our own custom styling.

You can see the full set of reset styles Tailwind uses by looking at the file, node_modules/tailwindcss/dist/base.css. Essentially, though, Preflight does a few things:

- It overrides all styling from headers, so for example, an h1 is visually identical to the base text.

- It removes styling from ul and ol lists, resulting in no bullets by default, which is an ironic thing to mention in a bulleted list.

- It sets all margins to zero for elements that would normally have margins.

- It sets all borders to a 0-pixel width, solid, and the defined border color by default.

- It gives buttons a default border.

- It sets images and image-like objects to display: block rather than display: inline, meaning they'll set themselves up as separate paragraphs (as if they were div tags) rather than inline (as if they were span tags).

If you only use the Preflight styles, you'll get a pretty boring page. But that's the point. Using Preflight ensures that any change to the display properties are affirmatively and explicitly added by us.

The @tailwind components file is small, and it only consists of the definitions of the container CSS classes, which are usually used at the top level of a page to define the box that the whole page is drawn in. I'll talk about this more in Chapter 5, Page Layout, on page 43.

The bulk of what's considered to be Tailwind is in the @tailwind utilities file, which defines all the utilities and their modified variants. I'll spend most of this book describing the contents of this file.

Duplication

A common concern when looking at Tailwind and the long sets of class lists you often need to accomplish your design goals is how to manage duplication. That is, if you need to type class="text-6xl font-bold text-blue-700" for every h1, as we did in Introduction, on page xi, isn't that a lot of typing that needs to be consistent every time you need an h1? What if your h1 design changes?

Managing Duplication in Code

Tailwind does have a way to manage CSS class list duplication, but you're also encouraged to see the duplication issue as part of your larger code setup, not only as a CSS issue. No matter what tool you're using to build your HTML markup, it likely has component or function mechanisms you're already using to reduce code duplication. When using Tailwind, it's a great idea to see your CSS class lists as part of that code.

For example, if you're using React, you have components. Many other client-side frameworks offer components as well. Rather than manage duplication in CSS, you could create React components with the common Tailwind classes:

```
export const Header = ({children}) => {
  return (
    <div className="text-6xl font-bold text-blue-700">
      {children}
    </div>
  )
}
export const SubHeader = ({children}) => {
  return (
    <div className="text-4xl font--semibold">
      {children}
    </div>
  )
}
export const SubSubHeader = ({children}) => {
  return (
    <div className="text-lg font-medium italic">
      {children}
    </div>
  )
}
```

Then you'd use this:

```
<Header>Cool Text</Header>
<SubHeader>Less Cool Text</SubHeader>
<SubSubHeader>Kind of boring text</SubSubHeader>
```

In plain JavaScript, you could also create a function that returns the list of Tailwind classes:

```
const title = () => { return "text-6xl font-bold text-blue-700" }
```

And in React you'd use this:

```
<Component className={title}>Cool Text</Component>
```

In Ruby on Rails, you can similarly define helper methods for lists of Tailwind classes:

```
def title
  "text-6xl font-bold text-blue-700"
end
```

Or you can define an ERB partial with a name like app/views/partials/_title.erb:

```
<div className="text-6xl font-bold text-blue-700">
  <%= yield %>
</div>
```

The yield is important here because it allows you to call the partial with a block containing children. The syntax is a little weird:

```
<%= render partial: "partials/_title" do %>
  <h2>Whatever</h2>
<%= end %>
```

The inside of the block contains arbitrary ERB code that's inserted in place of the yield.

If you don't like any of these syntax options and would rather have a CSS-based solution for duplication, Tailwind provides a CSS directive called @apply and a directive called @layer, which we'll take a look at next.

Using @apply for Duplication

The @apply directive lets you use Tailwind classes in the definition of other CSS selectors. So we can redefine our header classes in CSS like this:

```
@layer components {
  .title { @apply text-6xl font-bold }
  .subtitle { @apply text-4xl font-semibold }
  .subsubtitle { @apply text-lg font-medium italic }
}
```

And you can then use those like any other CSS classes:

```
<div class="title">Title</div>
```

The @layer directive can either be base, components, or utilities. As far as the browser is concerned, if you use @layer, the selectors are defined as part of whatever layer you declare, no matter where in your CSS files the selector definitions are actually located.

Using @layer components defines the selector as part of the components and before the utilities. This means if you combine one of our own definitions with a Tailwind utility, the utility wins, which is what we want. So we can define, say, an extra big title with:

```
<div class="title text-5xl">Title</div>
```

To understand why @layer is important, you need to know a general principle of CSS: all else being equal, if two CSS classes are trying to adjust the same underlying property, the one defined last wins. (If you're familiar with CSS, you know that there's also a principle of *specificity*, where the most specific definition wins, but because all the Tailwind utilities have the same specificity, that's not an issue here.)

In a CSS file, if you have two definitions for the same CSS selector that define the same property, the selector defined later in the file wins. In Tailwind, if you have two utility classes that define the same property, the one that's later in the list wins, so class="text-xl text-2xl" will give you text that's sized 2xl.

By defining a custom selector inside a layer, the selector is loaded at the end of that layer and before the next layer. This has some consequences for how custom CSS might interact with other Tailwind utilities or CSS. For example, we can make our definitions part of the HTML by using @apply on tags, not class selectors. In this case, we put the definition in the base layer:

```
@layer base {
  h1 { @apply text-4xl font-bold }
  h2 { @apply text-2xl font-semibold }
  h3 { @apply text-lg font-medium italic }
}
```

Here, we're redefining the h1, h2, and h3 elements directly, so we can use this:

```
<h1>Title</h1>
```

By being in the base layer, these definitions are before all utilities, so that `<h1 class="text-6xl">` behaves as you'd want, with the 6xl taking precedence. If the h1 was defined in the utilities layer, then the h1 would have precedence because it'd be defined later than the text-6xl. And because we've moved the layer to base, Tailwind will consider this part of the Preflight styles and define it before any components. Again, this placement allows you to mix tags, components, and utilities as expected.

This is all quite useful, and it allows you to effectively build up your own framework using Tailwind utilities as building blocks. But it helps to realize that you're, in fact, building up a framework and taking upon yourself all the attendant naming and maintenance responsibilities.

Modifiers

There's one more Tailwind feature to talk about before we get to the utility classes: modifiers.

Modifiers are Tailwind's way of using CSS pseudo-classes, pseudo-elements, and media queries in the HTML markup. For example, it's common to want objects to display differently when the user drags a mouse over them, which corresponds to the CSS pseudo-class, hover.

In Tailwind, you can define utilities in terms of CSS pseudo-classes by adding modifiers to other Tailwind utilities. If you want an anchor tag to have an underline when the mouse goes over it, you could do this:

```
<a class="hover:underline">Click me</a>
```

That's compact, reasonably straightforward to read, and defined along with the HTML so it's clear when it applies. You can use hover: with any Tailwind utility. You can even use hover: with an arbitrary CSS style as in hover:[mask-type:luminance]. You can also combine modifiers: hover:dark:underline.

As you'll see in Chapter 7, Responsive Design, on page 61, Tailwind also uses modifiers to allow different utilities to be invoked based on the width of the screen, so you could write class="sm:m-2 lg:m-4, and your element would grow a bigger margin as the screen gets wider. Tailwind defines more than two dozen modifiers,[1] and the resulting CSS is automatically generated by the Tailwind CLI when you use them.

You can even use the modifiers in conjunction with @apply. So @apply hover:underline is a legal way to define a new CSS class.

CSS Units

Most values in CSS that define length or width can take a number with a unit. Height and width definitions can also take a percentage. CSS defines two kinds of units: *absolute* and *relative*.

Absolute units are defined in terms of real-world units, so you could define a width as, say, 5in for inches. More commonly, you'll see px for pixels. In the long-ago time, a px represented one actual display pixel, but computer and phone displays are much denser now, and a CSS pixel is defined as 1/96 of an inch. (You know, the commonly used split of an inch into 96ths.) For fonts you'll often see points, as in font-size: 20pt. A point is 1/72 of an inch, which is a measurement that far predates computers.

In CSS, you're more likely to see relative units, of which the most common is em, which is the size of the element, as in width: 10em. It's common to define font size in relative terms, but because font-size: 1.5em would be a circular definition, for the purposes of typographical properties, em refers to the font-size of the parent, rather than the element being matched.

1.　https://tailwindcss.com/docs/hover-focus-and-other-states

If that's confusing—which it is—it's also unstable, because changing a font size can have weird downstream effects on anything defined with an em. A more stable alternative is rem, which is the font size of the root element and which defaults to 16 points in the Tailwind reset system. Most distances in Tailwind are either defined as a percentage or in terms of rem.

Now, let's look at what Tailwind gives us for our typographic styling needs.

CHAPTER 3

Typography

Odds are your web application is displaying text to a reader. Much of the design of a website is about the placement, size, weight, and layout of text. In this chapter, we'll look at how Tailwind lets you control the display of text.

Size and Shape

Perhaps the first thing you notice about text on a web page is its size and styling. Tailwind provides a series of utilities for each.

The effective default for text size is the text-base class, which defines the CSS properties font-size: 1rem and line-height: 1.5rem, meaning the font size for text-base is the same as the font size for the root element of your page, and the line height is 1.5 times that size. Tailwind provides a family of utilities, text-{size}, which includes two smaller steps, ten larger ones, and the base class, giving us thirteen sizes overall. Each step defines a font size and a line height, as listed in the table on page 20.

This is our first encounter with one of Tailwind's explicit design goals, which is to provide a consistent set of steps for a potentially infinite set of values. With the text-{size} family of utilities, Tailwind makes it easy to keep sizing and spacing consistent throughout the site. As mentioned in Utilities, on page 10, you can use square brackets to define an arbitrary value as the size, as in text-[20px]; you do need to include the unit as well as the number.

Font styling—your basic bold, italic, underline—is covered by a few different CSS properties, but from Tailwind's perspective, these styles are just utility classes: italic and not-italic, and underline and no-underline. You'd only use not-italic and no-underline if you want the text to have different characteristics under different states. This is usually tied to responsive behavior at different screen sizes, which we'll look at later in Chapter 7, Responsive Design, on page 61. You can also use overline and line-through.

Class	Font Size	Line Height
text-xs	0.75rem	1rem
text-sm	0.875rem	1.25rem
text-base	1rem	1.5rem
text-lg	1.125rem	1.75rem
text-xl	1.25rem	1.75rem
text-2xl	1.5rem	2rem
text-3xl	1.875rem	2.25rem
text-4xl	2.25rem	2.5rem
text-5xl	3rem	1
text-6xl	3.75rem	1
text-7xl	4.5rem	1
text-8xl	6rem	1
text-9xl	8rem	1

If you have underline, overline, or line-through specified, you can add an additional class to style the line. Your options are decoration-solid, decoration-double, decoration-dotted, decoration-dashed, and decoration-wavy, all of which basically do what they say they do. A pattern specifies the width of the decoration, decoration-{width}, where the default values are 0, 1, 2, 4, and 8 corresponding to width in pixels. There's also decoration-auto and decoration-from-font, or you can use an arbitrary measurement. A similar pattern, underline-offset-{width}, specifies the offset from the line and uses the same set of numerical values, plus auto. You can specify the color of the underline as well with the pattern decoration-{color}. (See the next section for what goes into the color placeholder.)

For bold fonts, CSS provides nine grades of boldness from 100 to 900; normal text is 400. Tailwind also provides nine utility classes, one for each grade:

font-hairline

font-thin

font-light

font-normal

font-medium

font-semibold

font-bold

font-extrabold

font-black

Not all fonts will have distinct lettering at all weights, but commonly used web fonts should. I don't know why Tailwind doesn't use font-weight-100, which would seem to be more consistent with other naming. You can get it to do so by changing the configuration, though (see Chapter 8, Customizing Tailwind, on page 67). You can also put in an arbitrary value, as in font-[1200].

You might also want to ensure the case of the text. For example, you might want a header to be all uppercase. Tailwind provides four utility classes for case, all of which wrap the CSS text-transform property to provide the behavior the utility name describes:

uppercase

lowercase

capitalize

normal-case

With these in hand, we can start to build up styles for our actual headers. The following is, more or less, the default styling for a popular CSS framework's title and subtitle defaults:

```
<h1 class="text-3xl font-semibold">Title</h1>
<h2 class="text-xl">Subtitle</h2>
```

This gives us a title that's 1.875rem (30-point type) with a line height of 2.5rem (36 points) and semibold, and a subtitle that's 1.25rem (20 points) at normal weight and a line height of 1.75rem. I often like my headers to be a little more attention-grabbing, so I might do something like this:

```
<h1 class="text-4xl font-bold">Title</h1>
<h2 class="text-2xl font-semibold">Subtitle</h2>
<h3 class="text-lg font-medium italic">Header</h3>
```

This gives us a slightly bolder and bigger title and subtitle, plus a third-level header that's a little bit bigger than regular text, a little bit bolder, and also italic. I might also add some spacing around the headers; we'll look at how to do this in Chapter 4, The Box, on page 29.

Remember that Tailwind's reset styles make it so that h1, h2, and so on have no default styling, so using those tags with Tailwind is a semantic note that the text is a header of some kind. It has no stylistic effect.

Right now, there's a good chance you're asking whether I'm seriously telling you it's a good idea to have to type text-lg font-medium italic every time you want a header. That's a lot of typing, it's on the cryptic side, and it's a lot of typing. See Duplication, on page 12, for ideas on how to manage duplication in Tailwind.

Color and Opacity

Tailwind lets you adjust the color and opacity of text.

Let's talk about color first. Tailwind offers hundreds of color utilities out of the box, and those utilities behave similarly across many different color-related families of classes.

Text colors are of the pattern text-{color}. There're three special colors: text-transparent, text-inherit, and text-current. The text-transparent class makes the text transparent, meaning you can see the background color through it. You can sometimes use this class for effect, especially with bg-clip-text, which makes the background match the shape of the text. The text-current and text-inherit options are both useful resets. text-inherit uses the color inherited from a parent. The text-current class uses the CSS currentColor, which is normally used to set other color properties to the same color as the text; for text itself it should behave the same as text-inherit.

Tailwind also defines text-black, which sets the color to #000000, and text-white, which sets the color to #ffffff.

Most of the time, though, Tailwind uses combined classes: .text-{color}-{level}. Tailwind sets 22 different colors by default at 10 different levels, from the lightest at 50 and then every multiple of 100 from 100 to the darkest at 900. Following are the default colors, grouped by similarity:

- Slate, Gray, Zinc, Neutral, Stone
- Red, Orange, Pink, Rose
- Amber, Yellow
- Lime, Green, Emerald, Teal
- Cyan, Sky, Blue,
- Indigo, Violet, Purple, Fuchsia

Any combination of color and level can be used, like .text-yellow-400 or .text-blue-200. I'm not going to put the exact RGB hex values for all eighty combinations, but you can see them online in the Tailwind documentation.[1] The Tailwind documentation describes the levels as "expertly-crafted," which I take to mean that they aren't automatically calculated.

Custom colors can be defined in the configuration file (see Chapter 8, Customizing Tailwind, on page 67), or you can do one-offs, such as text-[#34da33].

As you'll see, many prefixes use the same colors and levels throughout Tailwind.

---

1.   https://tailwindcss.com/docs/customizing-colors#default-color-palette

You can count on the default colors getting darker as the numbers increase, and you can take advantage of this for some subtle effects:

```
<div class="text-gray-300 hover:text-gray-700">
  Hi
</div>
```

This gives you lighter gray text that darkens when the user hovers over it. You can even turn this into a function that returns a string of classes. Here's the JavaScript version:

```
const hoverDarker = (color) => {
  return `text-${color}-300 hover:text-${color}-700`
}
```

But see Change Generated Classes, on page 74, for a reason why you might not want to use this exact implementation.

Now, let's talk about opacity. Changing the opacity makes colors more or less visible. Tailwind allows you to specify the opacity as an extension to the color declaration using the pattern, text-gray-300/50. What that means is to specify opacity, you add a slash and then the opacity level after the color. The list of default opacity levels is a little weird—it's every multiple of 10 between 0 and 100, plus 5, 25, 75, and 95. The number represents a percentage, so, text-gray-300/20 for 20% or text-gray-300/95 for 95%. You can use square brackets for an arbitrary value, as in text-gray-300/[42].

All the same color patterns can be used to specify the color of the text pointer using the pattern caret-{color}, as in caret-fuschia-300 or caret-current. This includes arbitrary colors with caret-[#ababab].

Color Patterns

 You'll see this pattern a few different times in Tailwind: a class name made up of a prefix followed by the same set of color and opacity options. You'll see this for borders (border-), background colors (bg-), and many other color-based CSS properties. Later, in Chapter 8, Customizing Tailwind, on page 67, you'll see that colors can be customized in one place, and the change will apply to all of the properties that use colors.

Alignment and Spacing

Several Tailwind classes are used to specify the horizontal alignment of text:

text-left

text-center

text-right

text-justify

They all change the CSS text-align property. The exact bounds of the alignment depend on the box the text is in. (I'll talk more about that in Chapter 4, The Box, on page 29.)

The CSS property for vertical alignment is vertical-align, and these are the Tailwind classes:

align-baseline

align-top

align-middle

align-bottom

align-text-top

align-text-bottom

align-sub

align-super

As with the horizontal alignment, exact positioning depends on the text box.

For line spacing, Tailwind has both a relative and an absolute option. The relative option starts with leading-none, which makes the line height exactly the size of the font. ("Leading" is the printing term for line height, and it rhymes with "wedding," not "beading.") That's normally going to feel a little tightly packed, and Tailwind lets you separate the line height with the following classes in order from most closely packed to farthest apart:

leading-tight

leading-snug

leading-normal (1.5 times the font size, usually your default)

leading-relaxed

leading-loose

The absolute option is based on rem, meaning it's derived from the root element size, not the size of the DOM element it's attached to. You've got leading-3 through leading-10, which takes us from 0.75rem to 2.5rem in 0.25 increments. You have the arbitrary option here, with something like leading-[4.3rem].

Next is the property CSS calls letter-spacing and Tailwind calls tracking. You've got tracking-normal, then two utilities for pushing the text closer together:

tracking-tight

tracking-tighter

Also, you have three utilities for making the letter spacing wider:

tracking-wide

tracking-wider

tracking-widest

These utilities can add nice effects on headers with big text.

Special Text

Tailwind allows you to use modifiers to match CSS pseudo-classes for a few different types of text that you might want to treat differently.

The modifier selection applies to text that has been selected by the user, so you can apply color (selection:bg-red-400) or other styling (selection:font-bold). The selection modifier, if applied to a parent element, will be carried through to all child elements.

If you are into newspaper or magazine style effects, Tailwind offers both first-line and first-letter modifiers. This seems most applicable for size and weight, as in first-letter:text-9xl first-letter:font-bold first-line:text-2xl and so on.

Also, Tailwind allows before: and after: as modifiers for the CSS before:: and after:: pseudo-classes, which allow you to insert content that doesn't show up in the DOM. In most cases, though, it's easier and more effective to use actual HTML spans to put the content in the right place rather than using the CSS before and after utilities.

Lists

Tailwind includes two sets of classes to manage <li> tags. The first is the style of the list: you've got list-disc (bulleted), list-decimal (numbered), and list-none. You can also choose whether the bullet or number is inside or outside the text box with list-inside and list-outside.

The special modifier marker: lets you apply a style to the bullet or number in a list. Likely you'd use this for color (marker:text-blue-300) or size (marker:text-2xl). A nice thing about the marker modifier is that it can be inherited: you can apply it to the ul or ol tag and it will automatically cover the included li tags.

Typography Plugin

If you want some legible defaults for basic typography of long text on your page, Tailwind provides an official typography plugin.[2]

To install the plugin, you first add the package:

```
$ yarn add @tailwindcss/typography
```

Then add it to the Tailwind configuration file, which now should have this plugins section:

```
module.exports = {
  plugins: [
    require('@tailwindcss/typography'),
  ],
}
```

You use the typography plugin by adding the CSS class prose to any element, like this:

```
<article class="prose">
  All your text
</article>
```

If you want to see what this looks like in more detail, you can visit my very own blog at https://noelrappin.com/blog, which uses this plugin.

To change the size, you use size modifiers, which you must use in conjunction with a class that already uses prose, like this:

```
<article class="prose prose-sm">
  All your text
</article>
```

The base size is 1rem or 16 points. These are the size modifiers:

-sm 14pt

-lg 18pt

-xl 20pt

-2xl 40pt

You can similarly specify using one of the different default gray scales, with prose prose-gray, prose prose-neutral, prose prose-slate, prose prose-stone, and prose prose-zinc.

A typical use case for the prose plugin is to surround a chunk of previously existing text or rendered markdown. In those cases, the markup inside the

---

2.   https://tailwindcss.com/docs/typography-plugin

prose block will likely have HTML elements that are dynamically generated in such a way where you can't get to the internal elements of the text. In that case, you can specifically customize the behavior of HTML elements within the prose block. The general pattern here is prose-{element}:{tailwind}, where element is an HTML element (most of your popular HTML elements for prose text will qualify) and tailwind is a Tailwind utility class. An example might be prose-h1:font-bold or prose-a:decoration-red-700. There's a special element header that matches all the header elements.

Tailwind Forms

Tailwind provides a series of useful defaults for forms using the @tailwindcss/forms plugin.[3] As with the typography plugin described earlier, to install the plugin, first add the package:

```
$ yarn add @tailwindcss/forms
```

Then add require('@tailwindcss/forms') to the Tailwind configuration file:

```
module.exports = {
  plugins: [
    require('@tailwindcss/forms'),
  ],
}
```

This will give reasonable styles to the basic form elements. (See https://tailwindcss-forms.vercel.app for a demo.) For input forms, the plugin uses the type attribute to affect sizing, so you do need to have type=text even for basic inputs for the styling to work. Note that the Tailwind forms aren't designed to be a finished work by themselves, but rather a better reset to start from when adding styling to your custom page.

Now that we've seen how typography works, let's place that text inside a box.

---

3. https://github.com/tailwindlabs/tailwindcss-forms

CHAPTER 4

The Box

Each HTML element in the DOM takes up a rectangle of space on the screen. Every browser's developer tools include a representation of that rectangle that looks like this:

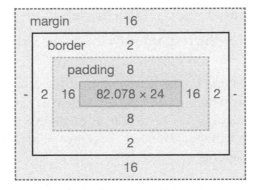

If you don't make any customizations, the size of the box is determined by the content of the element. Tailwind gives you control over every aspect of the box.

Can You See the Box?

Perhaps the most important feature of any DOM element is whether the user can see it. By manipulating this feature with a little JavaScript, you can add interaction cheaply. A common pattern is to load a lot of potential DOM elements at the initial page load but have many of them start off as hidden, manipulating visibility to change the page without needing to call the server for more data.

Most of the time when you want to have a DOM element the user can't see, you'll want to use the hidden Tailwind utility, which wraps the CSS property, display: none. In Tailwind, the opposite of hidden is usually block. While many other potential values for display are available, Tailwind's Preflight makes a lot of elements use the block value. The other common value is inline, but in Tailwind, you're more likely to construct inline behavior using a flexbox or grid layout (more on this in Chapter 5, Page Layout, on page 43).

Tailwind also has visible and invisible utilities. The difference between invisible and hidden is that a hidden element doesn't display and also isn't part of the DOM layout, and so its existence doesn't affect the layout of other elements. In contrast, an invisible element doesn't display its contents but does affect the layout of the rest of the page—it'll show up as a gap in the page, still sized, but empty.

What's in the Box?

The CSS box model has four parts. From inside out, they are:

- *Content*—Content is the text or media inside the element. (We looked at content in the previous chapter.)

- *Padding*—The padding is the space around the content but inside the border. You can specify the padding separately in each of the four directions, only horizontally, only vertically, or in all directions at once. I don't know you or your website, but odds are pretty good that a lot of your site could use more padding.

- *Border*—The border is the edge around your padding. The only thing that distinguishes border from padding is that you can use a color and a pattern to draw a border around the padding and content.

- *Margin*—The margin is outside the border and between this element and all the other elements. You can specify the margin in all directions the same way you can specify padding.

You can also specify the height and width of the box, either in absolute sizes or as a percentage of the available width and height. If you explicitly specify a width or height, any unused space is considered part of the content. If you do limit the size of the element, you can also tell the page what to do with any content that overflows that amount of size. Finally, you can do quite a few things with the background of an element.

Okay, let's talk about the parts of the box.

Padding and Margins

Padding and margins aren't next to each other—they're always separated by the border. But Tailwind handles them similarly enough that it's easy to talk about them together.

Tailwind provides, if I'm counting correctly, 245 different classes to manage padding (not counting arbitrary values). I'm not going to list them all here (though the Tailwind documentation[1] does), because there's a pattern to them: p{direction}-{size}.

All the padding classes start with p, followed by an optional character for the direction. Six directions exist: t, b, l, and r for top, bottom, left, and right, respectively; x for horizontal (meaning left and right); and y for vertical (meaning top and bottom). If there's no direction character, the padding appears in all directions.

By default, Tailwind defines 34 numerical sizes that can be used for padding and margins. A special size, px, is equal to 1 pixel:

0, 0.5, 1, 1.5, 2, 2.5, 3, 3.5, 4, 5, 6, 7, 8, 9, 10, 11, 12, 14, 16, 20, 24, 28, 32, 36, 40, 44, 48, 52, 56, 60, 64, 72, 80, 96

Each number corresponds to 0.25rem—or one-fourth of the size of the root element of the page.

For example, .p-10 is 2.5rem of padding in all directions, .px-4 is 1rem of padding horizontally, .pr-1.5 is 0.375rem of padding on the right, and .pt-px is 1 pixel of padding on top. The goal here is to give you more fine-grained control at small sizes and then a consistent set of values for higher amounts of padding. You can have multiple padding classes for different directions, such as class="px-10 py-20".

Sizing Pattern

 This sizing pattern is another Tailwind pattern that's used for several different properties. We see it here for padding as in p-24, but it's also used for margin (m-24), height (h-24), and width (w-24). In all cases, you can use square brackets for an arbitrary size and unit, as in p-[15px].

Margins follow the same basic structure as padding with a few changes:

- Margin classes start with an m, and the pattern is m{direction}-{size}. Like padding, you can specify multiple margins in different directions.

---

1. https://tailwindcss.com/docs/padding

- All directions have an additional size option: -auto. Auto is the margin option that horizontally centers the element within its parent container. You can do an auto on the top and bottom, but it doesn't have any effect. (We'll look at how to vertically center elements in Chapter 5, Page Layout, on page 43.)

- Margins can be negative, which moves an element closer to the next element than it otherwise would be, rather than farther away, placing it inside the margin of the element next to it. A negative margin starts with -m instead of m and has the same direction and size options as regular margins.

Borders

Borders are similar to margins and padding but are more complicated because they can have their own color and style.

The size options for borders are more limited because you typically don't want borders to be as big as margins might get. More importantly, the size options for borders are measured in pixels, not rem. The most basic border option is simply border, which gives you a 1-pixel border in all four directions.

After that you have .border-{side}-{size}, where the side is optional. But unlike padding and margins, a dash is included before the side. The side options are: -b, -t, -l, and -r, and -x and -y, which combine two sides. Not including a side applies the size to all four sides. The size is also optional: -0, -2, -4, and -8, which is the width of the border in pixels. No specified size means a size of 1. Arbitrary values can be used with square brackets.

If either the side or the size isn't included, you don't need the prefixing dash. For example, valid border width classes include: border-2, which doesn't specify a side and gives you a 2-pixel border on all sides; border-b, which doesn't specify a size and gives you a 1-pixel bottom border; and border-r-4, which results in a 4-pixel right border.

Border lines may have a style, for which you'd use a separate Tailwind utility class. The default is a solid border, which is indicated with border-solid. Tailwind also provides utilities for border-dashed, border-dotted, border-double, and border-none.

Border lines may also have a color and an opacity. The border color and opacity options are exactly the same as the text color options, only prefixed with border. For example, you can specify color with border-{color}, as in border-gray-500, and add an opacity with border-gray-500/50. The colors and opacity levels are the same as for text. You can specify border color on a specific side by adding the same side modifiers, as in border-r-gray-500 or border-x-gray-500.

Finally, borders may be round. Tailwind provides the following nine basic rounded options, each of which specifies the radius size in rem:

Class	Radius Size
rounded-none	Specifies a radius of 0, for no rounding at all
rounded-sm	0.125rem
rounded	0.25rem
rounded-md	0.375rem
rounded-lg	0.5rem
rounded-xl	0.75rem
rounded-2xl	1rem
rounded-3xl	1.5rem
rounded-full	Sets the border radius to effectively infinity (okay, 9999 pixels) allowing for something to look like a circle rather than a rounded rectangle
rounded-[{size}]	Allows you to specify an arbitrary radius with a unit

You might want to round only one or two corners. The only case I can think of for this offhand is if you have a lot of elements grouped together into a larger rounded rectangle. If you want, you can insert a direction between rounded and the size. You can specify both corners on a side with a direction of b, t, l, or r. You can also specify a single corner with tl, tr, bl, or br. Legal options might include rounded-tr-md or rounded-b-full. Here's a small example of some of the margin and border options (see also the image on page 34):

```
html/box.html
<div>
  <div class="mb-10">
    <button class="p-10 border border-black">One</button>
    <button class="m-10 border border-black">Two</button>
    <button class="m-2 p-2 border-4 border-black">Three</button>
  </div>
  <div>
    <button class="m-4 p-4 border-2 border-black rounded-md">
      Four
    </button>
    <button class="m-4 p-4 border-2 border-black rounded-2xl">
      Five
    </button>
    <button class="m-4 p-4 border-2 border-black rounded-full">
      Six
    </button>
  </div>
</div>
```

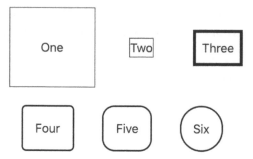

In the top row, the first button specifies padding and a border outside the padding, while the second button specifies a margin, and the border is inside the margin. The bottom row of buttons shows different rounded radius options.

Tailwind has a different way to specify a border called a *ring*. Rings have advantages over borders. For one thing, they actually look good and work well on rounded elements. Also, rings are implemented using CSS box shadow properties, so they don't affect layout spacing.

Rings can have width, color, opacity, and an optional offset. If color isn't specified, the default color is a not-fully opaque blue, which makes it look like the button has focus. The pattern is ring-{width}, where the width is 0, 1, 2, 4, and 8, corresponding to the pixel width of the ring (like a border). There's also simply ring, which is three pixels, and ring-inset, which draws the ring in the content part of the box, rather than the border part of the box, and you can use ring-[{arbitrary}] with an arbitrary size and unit.

The pattern ring-{color} works with any defined color to change the color of the ring, and adding a slash, as in ring-{color}/{opacity}, changes the opacity, again with the same levels as text opacity. ring-offset-{pixels} offsets the ring slightly, and ring-offset-{color} gives the offset ring a color. Here's an example:

html/box.html
```
<div>
  <button class="m-4 p-4 rounded-md ring">Four</button>
  <button class="m-4 p-4 rounded-2xl ring-2">Five</button>
  <button
    class="m-4 p-4 rounded-full ring-4 ring-offset-4 ring-offset-black"
  >
    Six
  </button>
</div>
```

Background Color

Tailwind's background color is similar to text color and border color: the pattern is bg-{color}, and uses the same color names as the other groups (bg-red-700 or bg-orange-300). Tailwind also provides bg-{color}/{opacity} with the same steps as text opacity. As in other places, you can use arbitrary values via square brackets for the color (bg-[#cdcdcd]) or the opacity (bg-red-700/[43]).

Shadows

Technically, a box shadow isn't a background color, but it's sort of used like one. Tailwind provides a few utilities to manage the box shadow. The base utility, shadow, effectively creates a 10% opacity black border that's 1-pixel vertically offset, with a 3-pixel width. You can then make that smaller with the xs and sm modifiers or bigger with the md, lg, xl, and 2xl modifiers (shadow-sm, shadow-xl, and so on). Note that arbitrary values here are more complicated than in other Tailwind patterns. (See https://tailwindcss.com/docs/box-shadow for details.) The color of the shadow can be specified with shadow-{color}.

Separately, you can have a small inset shadow with the shadow-inner class, which makes the element look like it's lower than the rest of the screen. (Sorry, no size variants.) And you can cancel all of these with shadow-none. As you can see in the following example, it's a pretty subtle effect unless you make it large (see also the image on page 36):

```
html/box.html
<div class="bg-gray-50 p-10">
  <div class="mb-10">
    <button class="p-10 mx-10 shadow-sm bg-white">One</button>
    <button class="p-10 mx-10 shadow-sm bg-white">Two</button>
    <button class="p-10 mx-10 shadow-lg bg-white">Three</button>
  </div>
  <div>
    <button class="p-10 mx-10 shadow-xl bg-white">Four</button>
    <button class="p-10 mx-10 shadow-2xl bg-white">Five</button>
    <button class="p-10 mx-10 shadow-inner bg-white">Six</button>
  </div>
</div>
```

Tailwind also provides support for the drop shadow filter. The difference between box shadows and drop shadows is subtle; for our purposes the biggest difference is that the drop shadow will work better if the element is not rectangular (for example, if it's an image with a transparent background). You can get a drop shadow with drop-shadow and use the same size modifiers that are used by the regular shadow.

One	Two	Three

Four	Five	Six

Gradients

Tailwind also lets you set the background as a gradient, which requires you to specify multiple classes on the same element. I think this is the first time we've seen a case where you need multiple Tailwind classes to get something to work right, which is a pattern we'll see more frequently as we look at page layout options in the next chapter.

In pure CSS, you specify a gradient by assigning the background-image: property a value from a linear-gradient function. You specify a direction, a "from" color (which is the starting point of the gradient), and a "to" color (which is the ending point). Optionally, you can specify a "via" color, which is a middle point.

Tailwind provides utilities with the pattern, bg-gradient-to-{direction}, and the four sides as directions: t, b, r, and l. So bg-gradient-to-t means the gradient "from" color starts at the bottom and shades to the "to" color, which is at the top, while bg-gradient-to-r means that the "from" color is at the left, and the "to" color is at the right.

You also get four corner directions: tl, tr, bl, and br, which combine to provide a diagonal gradient. So bg-gradient-to-tr is a gradient going diagonally from bottom left to top right.

bg-none clears the gradient.

With the direction set, we can then add in the colors. We use the same color names we've already seen, but with the prefixes from-, to-, and via-. To go from red to blue and right to left, you'd need three classes:

bg-gradient-to-l from-red-500 to-blue-500

If you want to stop at yellow in the middle, you'd add a "via":

bg-gradient-to-l from-red-500 to-blue-500 via-yellow-500

If you specify a "from" or both "from" and "via" without specifying a "to" color, the gradient will shade toward transparent.

Because this book isn't printed in color, I have limited options for showing the true effects of a gradient, but here's an example in grayscale:

```
html/box.html
<div>
  <div class="mb-10 bg-gradient-to-r from-gray-50 to-black p-10 w-1/2">
    <button class="p-10 mx-10 bg-white">One</button>
    <button class="p-10 mx-10 bg-white">Two</button>
  </div>
  <div
    class="mb-10 p-10 w-1/2
           bg-gradient-to-r from-gray-50 via-black to-gray-50">
    <button class="p-10 mx-10 bg-white">Three</button>
    <button class="p-10 mx-10 bg-white">Four</button>
  </div>
</div>
```

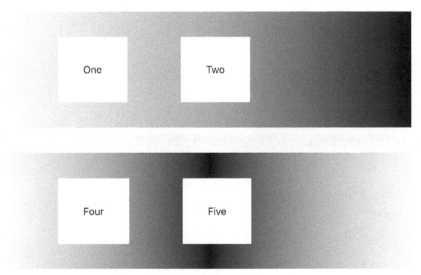

Background Images

CSS has a lot of properties for displaying a background image, and Tailwind provides utilities for almost all of them.

Specifying Images

If you want a background image that comes from a URL, Tailwind provides utilities for how that image is displayed but not for the URL itself. You have three options for specifying the background image URL: you can use the style= attribute of the DOM element, as in , or you can use the arbitrary syntax and surround it in square brackets, as in class="[background-image:url({url})]". Finally, you can create your own CSS utility classes:

```
.bg-pattern-image {
  background-image: url(whatever);
}
```

Positioning

When you have a background image, you can specify how the background image is positioned in the box. This tells CSS which side of the image should touch which side of the box. Tailwind provides nine utilities. The first one centers the image in the center of the box:

bg-center

Eight directions exist, including four sides:

bg-left

bg-right

bg-top

bg-bottom

And four corner utilities:

bg-left-top

bg-left-bottom

bg-right-bottom

bg-right-top

I'm genuinely not sure why the horizontal side goes first here when the vertical side has gone first in all the other instances when we've talked about corners. Nor do I know why they're spelled out.

Tiling

If the image is smaller than the box, you have the option to tile it. bg-repeat tiles the image horizontally and vertically. To go in only one direction, you'd use bg-repeat-x or bg-repeat-y. The utility bg-no-repeat resets everything.

Two special options, bg-repeat-round and bg-repeat-space, change how the tiling places the images. The default repeat will put a partial image at the end of the box. If you choose bg-repeat-space, there will be no partial image and any whitespace will be distributed evenly between the tiled images. If you choose bg-repeat-round, there will be no whitespace because each image will be stretched to cover the whitespace.

Scrolling

A common effect is to hold the background in place when the page scrolls so the viewport shows a different part of the image as the user scrolls through. Tailwind lets you do this with bg-fixed; the opposite of which is bg-local or bg-scroll, depending on whether you want a scroll bar in the viewport itself or not.

Location

You can specify the part of the box that will contain the image. The default is bg-clip-padding, where the background image displays in the content and padding parts of the box but not in the border. You can also make the image cover the border with bg-clip-border, or you can limit the image to only the content and not the padding with bg-clip-content.

More interestingly, bg-clip-text shows only the background image inside the shape of the content text. You'll want to combine this with text-transparent so the text color won't block it, but then you can see the background color or image only in the text. If you combine this with gradients, you get a text gradient as shown in this example:

```
html/box.html
<div class="bg-gray-50">
  <div class="text-6xl font-bold p-10">
    <div
      class="bg-clip-text text-transparent py-2
             bg-gradient-to-l from-gray-50 to-black">
    NorthBy: A Premium in Sight and Sound
    </div>
  </div>
</div>
```

NorthBy: A Premium in Sight and Sound

Filters

CSS defines a lot of filters that affect the display of an element. Tailwind allows you to use them; here's a set of the most useful.

You can blur the element with blur and blur the background with bg-blur. Technically, that's an 8-pixel blur. Tailwind provides one smaller blur, blur-sm, and four larger ones, blur-md, blur-xl, blur-2xl, and blur-3xl (adding bg- to any of these works for background only).

You can make an element grayscale with grayscale and negate it with grayscale-0. Similarly, you can make an element sepia toned with sepia and negate it with sepia-0.

You can adjust the brightness of an element with brightness-{level}, where the level can be 0, 50, 75, 90, 95, 100, 105, 110, 125, 150, or 200, where brightness-100 is 100%, or neutral. Similarly, you can adjust the contrast with contrast level, but the standard values are just 0, 50, 75, 100, 125, 150, and 200. Finally, you can saturate with saturate-{level}, which has even fewer defaults—just 0, 50, 100, 150, and 200. Arbitrary values can be used with square brackets for all three of these utilities.

Height and Width

The height and width of elements are notoriously difficult to manage in CSS. Tailwind provides some utilities for sizing, but remember that sizing is also often dependent on the available size based on both the parent elements and the content.

Tailwind uses the patterns w-{size} and h-{size} for the width and height utility classes. For both directions, Tailwind offers a set of fixed size options based on the same sizing scale and the same set of numbers we've seen for padding and margins, with each number corresponding to 0.25rem.

Special options include these:

-auto   auto-sizing
-px   single pixel
-full   100% of the parent container
-screen   100% of the viewport
-min   minimum content size (CSS min-content)
-max   maximum content size (CSS max-content)
-fit   fit content size (CSS fit-content)

You can use these in classes like h-0, w-8, or h-px.. The -min content sizes the box to the smallest amount that content can be in; -max content goes to the widest amount; and -fit content is the widest amount that fits between the min-content and max-content.

A series of relative width options are also available. Tailwind gives you a series of fractional options, such as .w-1/2 for 50%. You get fractions for halves, thirds, quarters, fifths, sixths, and twelfths (twelfths only exist for width, not height). All of these are actual Tailwind utility classes: .w-3/4, .h-2/6, .w-7/12. You can use these widths to fake a grid layout, but it's easier to use an actual grid layout, as you'll see in Chapter 5, Page Layout, on page 43.

CSS also allows you to specify the minimum and maximum height and width, and Tailwind gives you limited utilities for them. On the minimum side, you have .min-h-0 and .min-h-full, and .min-w-0 and min-w-full, giving you a minimum size of zero or of the entire parent container. You also have -min, -max, and -fit as suffixes for both.

For height, you also have a viewport option: .min-h-screen.

On the maximum side, for height, you have max-h-{size}, with all the same list of size numbers, plus .max-h-full and .max-h-screen for the full parent container height or the full screen height, respectively.

Maximum width has different options. You have max-w-0 for zero width, and max-w-none for no width, which are different things in CSS. There are a bunch of size options, max-w-{size}, where the size is xs, sm, md, lg, xl, 2xl, up through 7xl. The xs option is 20rem, the 7xl option is 80rem.

You'll find a special option for text, max-w-prose, which is 65 characters wide. There's a 100% of parent option, .max-w-full. You also have screen options based on screen size: .max-w-screen-sm, .max-w-screen-md, .max-w-screen-lg, .max-w-screen-xl, and .max-w-screen-2xl. (I'll talk more about the screen widths in Chapter 7, Responsive Design, on page 61.)

Now that we've got our boxes set, let's talk about laying out entire pages.

CHAPTER 5

Page Layout

In the previous chapter, we looked at ways you can use Tailwind to control the display of a single DOM element. In this chapter, we'll look at how Tailwind can manage the layout of multiple elements.

With Tailwind, you can lay out the elements on an entire page and manage common features like navigation, sidebars, and footers. You can also use Tailwind to put together complex groupings of elements within a page, such as cards or hero blocks.

Let's start with some general utilities Tailwind provides to help place elements on a page: the box-to-box relationships.

Containers

Many CSS frameworks use a container class as the general top-level container to specify page width. While Tailwind does offer a container utility, Tailwind's version does much less than similar classes do in other frameworks. All the container utility does in Tailwind is specify the max-width of the element based on the width of the browser viewport. For example, any viewport between 640 and 768 pixels wide would be set to a max-width of 640 pixels. Once the viewport goes over 768, the max-width stays at 768 pixels until the viewport hits 1024 pixels and then jumps again when the viewport reaches 1280 pixels.

The advantage of using a container is that it allows you to only worry about those specific widths in your design rather than having to take into account any possible width the viewport might have.

Viewports

In CSS, the viewport is the area of the browser where the user can see content. Usually, the dimension of concern is the width of the viewport because that determines how much content can be placed across the screen without scrolling horizontally. The HTML meta tag is used to control the viewport width on mobile screens. By default, mobile browsers often assume a wider display than the actual device (often 980 pixels) and scale the content to fit on screen. That usually looks terrible. You should use the content= "width=device-width,initial-scale=1" attribute for the browser to use the device size as the viewport rather than scaling the display down from a wider size.

If you're familiar with other frameworks, Tailwind's container won't have features you may be expecting. A Tailwind container doesn't automatically horizontally center its child elements. To get centering behavior, you pair the container with mx-auto. A Tailwind container also doesn't introduce a padding or margin to pull its elements away from the browser's border. To get this behavior, you pair the container with an m- or p- utility. So a plausible class list for your top-level element might be class="container mx-auto py-12 px-6".

Floats and Clears

Although a fresh new design will likely use the grid and flexbox tools described in the rest of this chapter to position elements, if you're using Tailwind in a legacy project, you might still need to deal with floats and clearfixes.

In CSS, the float property positions content inside its container. Typically, the float property is used to position a particular element, often an image, to one side or the other of its container, allowing the rest of the container, often text, to stay completely on the other side, rather than mixing the elements together.

Tailwind provides float-left and float-right for positions, and float-none as a reset option.

The CSS clear property forces an element to be placed below any elements it might otherwise overlap with on one or both sides. (Technically, it prevents other elements from floating, which amounts to the same thing.) Tailwind provides utilities to specify a clear behavior on either side, both sides, or no sides: clear-left, clear-right, clear-both, and clear-none.

Position and Z-Index

In CSS, the z-index property is an integer determining how items stack on top of each other along what would be the "z axis" if you ran an axis outward perpendicular to the screen. Tailwind provides the pattern, z-{index}, where the index can be 0, 10, 20, 30, 40, 50, or auto. You can use a negative z-index of those values by using the -z pattern, -z-20, or with an arbitrary value z-[-1].

Tables

The classic way of spacing HTML pages is the table. Unless you're actually displaying tabular data, a CSS grid is now preferable for layout purposes, so Tailwind doesn't provide many specific table utilities.

Tailwind lets you use table-auto to keep the default browser behavior of auto-spacing the columns of a table based on its content. If you want to explicitly specify column widths, you can use table-fixed on the <table> element and then put an explicit width helper on each column of the table—the fractional helpers are useful for this:

```
html/page.html
<table class="table-fixed border border-collapse">
  <tr>
    <th class="border border-black w-1/6">Small</th>
    <th class="border border-black w-2/6">Medium</th>
    <th class="border border-black w-3/6">Large</th>
  </tr>
</table>
```

Small	Medium	Large

Tailwind also lets you merge the borders of adjacent table cells with the help of the border-collapse utility, which is reset with border-separate.

Tailwind offers the odd: or even: modfier to give tables alternating row colors, such as class="odd:bg-white even:bg-grey-300", for example.

Grids

One of the great innovations of the first round of CSS frameworks was support for a grid layout where you could easily place things on a 12-column grid. The existence of grid spacing made page layout much easier. Over time, the frameworks became even more flexible and eventually grid support was built directly into CSS.

Grids are still great for a lot of layout choices, and Tailwind offers useful utilities for setting up a grid layout using the CSS grid properties. First, there's grid, which is a utility for the CSS property, display: grid. You need the grid utility as part of the class list at the top level of your grid, above the individual elements of the grid.

Once you've created a grid element, you can use Tailwind to specify the number of rows or columns in that grid. You can also adjust the behavior of individual elements in the grid. You can specify a start or end point for an element in the grid, specify the span of rows or columns the element takes up, or change the spacing of each element inside the grid.

The most common use of a grid is to separate the page into a series of columns, which you can do in Tailwind with the grid-cols-{count} helpers. These go from .grid-cols-1 to .grid-cols-12, each of which separates the page into that many columns. The reset out of grid-land is grid-cols-none.

Unlike some other CSS grid frameworks, you don't need to explicitly specify a row. Inside a grid, CSS will autofill down to the next row based on the number of columns you declare. For example, you can use something like this:

```
html/page.html
<div class="grid grid-cols-2 w-1/4 gap-4">
  <div class="border bg-gray-300 text-center">A</div>
  <div class="border bg-gray-300 text-center">B</div>
  <div class="border bg-gray-300 text-center">C</div>
  <div class="border bg-gray-300 text-center">D</div>
</div>
```

You wind up with a 2x2 grid with A and B on the top row and C and D on the bottom row, like this:

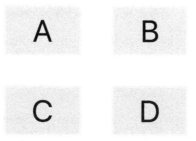

A cool feature of CSS grids that's hard to do in some of the other CSS frameworks is that you can use a 90-degree twist by specifying the number of rows. In Tailwind, this is done with the grid-rows-{count} helper, which can have a suffix of 1 to 12 or none.

You can also specify the direction in which data flows through the grid. The default, grid-flow-row, causes elements inside the grid to flow horizontally in rows, as you saw in the earlier example. This is the normal behavior of DOM elements that you're probably familiar with.

Or you can use grid-flow-col, in which case elements in the grid fill vertically column by column, like so:

```
html/page.html
<div class="grid grid-rows-2 w-1/4 gap-4 grid-flow-col">
  <div class="border bg-gray-300 text-center">A</div>
  <div class="border bg-gray-300 text-center">B</div>
  <div class="border bg-gray-300 text-center">C</div>
  <div class="border bg-gray-300 text-center">D</div>
</div>
```

This gives you a 2x2 grid, but the A and B are the left column, while C and D are the right column, like this:

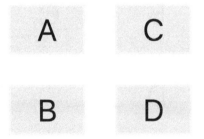

As you can see in the previous examples, you can add a gap between table cells with the conveniently named gap-{size} helper, which takes a suffix that's the size of the gap, using the same "some numbers from 0 to 96 and also px" measurement scheme we saw for padding and margins. If you want the gap sizing to only be horizontal, you can use gap-x-{size}. And if you want the gap to only be vertical, use gap-y-{size}.

Span

As with CSS tables, sometimes you want a cell to cover more than one row or column. Tailwind offers two ways to manage this: span and start/end.

Using span, you specify the number of columns or rows you want the cell to take up with col-span-{count} or row-span-{count}, where the suffix is the number of columns or rows. The default then is col-span-1 or row-span-1. The reset helpers are col-span-auto and row-span-auto.

The important part is that the flow behavior still continues. If you add a span to the first element, our four-cell example is this:

```
html/page.html
<div class="grid grid-cols-2 w-1/4 gap-4">
  <div class="border bg-gray-300 text-center col-span-2">A</div>
  <div class="border bg-gray-300 text-center">B</div>
  <div class="border bg-gray-300 text-center">C</div>
  <div class="border bg-gray-300 text-center">D</div>
</div>
```

You get this as a result:

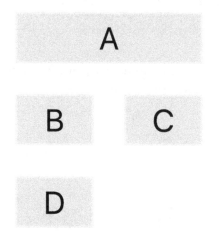

You can also span elements row-wise:

```
html/page.html
<div class="grid grid-cols-2 w-1/4 gap-4">
  <div class="border bg-gray-300 text-center row-span-2">A</div>
  <div class="border bg-gray-300 text-center">B</div>
  <div class="border bg-gray-300 text-center">C</div>
  <div class="border bg-gray-300 text-center">D</div>
</div>
```

The result looks like this:

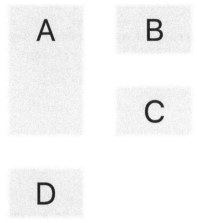

Start/End

You can adjust the placement of a grid item by specifying its start and end with col-start-{column} and col-end-{column} or row-start-{row} and row-end-{row}, where the suffix is either the number of the location or the reset value, auto. The key points are that the lowest start location is 1 and the end location is exclusive, meaning it's not part of the item. Declaring an item as class="col-start-2 col-end-4" means the element will encompass column 2 and column 3, but not column 4.

By default, the start and end locations are automatically determined by the placement of the previous items in the grid, and the span is 1. You can specify any two of the start, end, and span items, and the layout will work. For example, class="col-span-3, col-end-5" would take up columns 2, 3, and 4, spanning 3 columns and ending before the fifth column.

Columns

If you want a more classic magazine layout, you can use column flow, which is also suitable for photo layouts.

You specify column layouts in Tailwind in one of two ways. You can specify any number of columns from 1 to 12 with the pattern column-{count}. Alternately, you can specify the column by width with column-{size}, where the columns range from 2xs to xs, sm, md, lg, xl, and then 2xl through 7xl. The widths range irregularly from 16rem to 80rem, and you can specify an arbitrary width with the square bracket notation column-[{size}]. Using column-auto resets the columns. Just as with grids, you can use the gap family of classes to separate the columns.

Flexbox

Flexbox is a different way to arrange multiple related elements. Where a grid is designed as a two-dimensional layout, a flexbox layout is one-dimensional, placing items one after another in a row or column.

I realize that sounds less useful than a full grid.

But flexbox is likely to be more useful to you than a grid layout for three reasons:

- A flexbox container has better controls for dynamically managing the size of elements.

- Although a flexbox container is conceptually a single row, it can be made to automatically wrap its contents on the screen when the contents get too wide.

- Flexbox containers can be nested, meaning you can start with a flexbox row, but elements inside that row could themselves be flexbox columns, which in turn could contain flexbox rows. Nesting flexboxes gives you a lot of options for controlling layout.

Grids are still useful for managing content that's tabular in nature, which is true of some data display but not true of every kind of layout.

Think about a common page structure, where you have a full-width header, below that a left and right sidebar with main content in the middle, and below that, a full-width footer.

You could think of that layout as a grid: the header is the first row of the grid that has one element with a column span of three. The second row has three elements for the sidebars and the main content, width-adjusted, and the third row has another element with a column span of 3, like this:

```
html/page.html
<div class="grid grid-cols-3 gap-4 w-1/3">
  <div class="text-center col-span-3">Header</div>
  <div class="text-center w-1/5">Left Sidebar</div>
  <div class="text-center w-3/5">Content</div>
  <div class="text-center w-1/5">Right Sidebar</div>
  <div class="text-center col-span-3">Footer</div>
</div>
```

That's not bad, but you can also think of the layout as a flexbox. Your flexbox could be a column with three elements, whose second element is a row with three elements, like this (we'll look at what these utilities mean in a second):

```
html/page.html
<div class="flex flex-col w-1/3">
  <div class="flex-grow">Header</div>
  <div class="flex flex-row">
    <div class="text-center w-1/5">Left Sidebar</div>
    <div class="text-center w-3/5">Content</div>
    <div class="text-center w-1/5">Right Sidebar</div>
  </div>
  <div class="flex-grow">Footer</div>
</div>
```

Or, you can think of the page as a single row that happens to wrap like this:

```
html/page.html
<div class="flex flex-row flex-wrap w-1/3">
  <div class="w-full">Header</div>
  <div class="text-center w-1/5">Left Sidebar</div>
  <div class="text-center w-3/5">Content</div>
  <div class="text-center w-1/5">Right Sidebar</div>
  <div class="w-full">Footer</div>
</div>
```

All three of these approaches will give you more or less this layout:

Header

Left   Content   Right

Sidebar   Sidebar

Footer

It turns out that the flexbox is more, well, flexible than a grid. In particular, flexbox layouts are much easier to adapt to different screen sizes.

Direction and Axis

The foundation of how a flexbox lays out elements is its direction, which you set with Tailwind utilities. The direction can be either horizontal, with flex-row, or vertical, with flex-column. You can go backward in your flow with flex-row-reverse and flex-col-reverse. The axis in the direction of the flow is referred to as the *main axis*, while the other direction is referred to as the *cross axis*.

In Tailwind, the parent flexbox container must include the class, flex (in the same way grids need to have the class, grid).

An important thing to know about the row direction is that it's not necessarily left to right; the rows flow in the direction of the text. So, if you internationalize your text to, say, Hebrew, all your flexboxes will automatically flip direction. The column's main axis is always top to bottom.

Order and Wrap

The next most important property of the flexbox is whether it'll wrap, which is a property of the parent of the box. The default is not to wrap, flex-no-wrap, but if you specify flex-wrap, then your row container will automatically move items to the next row if the item would overflow the main axis of the container. Normally, that'd be going over the width of a row flexbox, but you could also explicitly set the height of a column box and have it wrap. If for some reason you're living in the Upside Down, Tailwind provides flex-wrap-reverse.

You can explicitly specify the order of the elements in the flexbox with the order-{integer} utility, where the suffix is any integer from 1 to 12, or you can use order-first, order-last, or order-none. This is also a good place for the arbitrary value syntax, if you have more than twelve items, such as order-[42]. If the order is specified for one or more elements in the flexbox, then that order property determines where in the box that element goes, overriding the order in which the element appears in the source HTML.

One great use of this property is to allow the main content to come before the other elements in the source order but still display correctly. This code provides the same layout as the snippet shown earlier:

```
html/page.html
<div class="flex flex-row flex-wrap w-1/3">
  <div class="text-center w-3/5 order-3">Content</div>
  <div class="w-full order-1">Header</div>
  <div class="text-center w-1/5 order-2">Left Sidebar</div>
  <div class="text-center w-1/5 order-4">Right Sidebar</div>
  <div class="w-full order-5">Footer</div>
</div>
```

A reason why you'd want to do that is to allow an adaptive screen reader to get to the content quickly while still allowing the visual display of the page to place the content in the middle.

Grow, Shrink…Flex

The "flex" in flexbox comes from the ability of a flexbox container to change the size and placement of its items dynamically. Tailwind gives you access to common defaults. These are properties that are placed on the elements inside a flexbox, not on the parent.

If you want to specify the size of an element within a flexbox, you can use the basis-{size} Tailwind classes, which use the CSS flex-basis property. Flex basis specifies the element's size along the main axis of the flex, meaning width for row boxes, and height for column boxes. If set, flex basis will be used instead of the applicable width or height properties for elements inside a flexbox. The size options for basis are almost the same as the options for width. You have the same set of standard numbers with a low of zero and a high of 80 plus fractions for halves, thirds, quarters, fifths, sixths, and twelfths, plus auto, px, and full, so basis-4 or basis-3/5, or basis-auto. And remember that you have the option for arbitrary values, as in basis-[20px].

If a specific width isn't specified, a flexbox will grow or shrink the items within it to fill the available space. If you don't want a specific item to grow or shrink, you specify it as flex-none, which will keep it at its default size. If you want the item to be able to grow or shrink as needed to fill the available size of the container, you use flex-auto or flex-1. The difference between the two is that flex-auto starts with each element's default size and then increases or decreases size for each element that's able to grow or shrink, whereas flex-1 resets each item to zero size and equally assigns space to all items, regardless of their natural size. In general, using flex-1 on a set of items will give you equally sized items, and flex-auto won't.

You can choose to specify shrink behavior without touching grow behavior. To allow shrinking, use flex-shrink, and to prevent shrinking, use flex-shrink-0. Similarly, flex-grow and flex-grow-0 allow and prevent element growth without affecting shrink behavior.

Box Alignment

In addition to using flexbox to place items on the page, Tailwind includes utilities that allow you to be more specific about the alignment and justification of elements within the flexbox. These utilities also work for grid layouts, where appropriate.

I talked about how a flexbox container has a main axis and a cross axis. The Tailwind utilities that affect placement along the main axis all start with justify-, and utilities that affect placement across the cross axis don't. These names are chosen to match the names of the underlying CSS properties.

Main Axis

Let's look at the main axis first. Item placement can be specified along the main axis in two ways: placement of the item along the main axis of the entire flexbox, and placement of an individual item along the main axis of its own box within the flexbox container. Both of these placements can be defined separately and include utilities that are properties of the parent flexbox container, not individual elements.

When placing elements along the main axis, Tailwind includes utilities for how items are placed if the total width of the items is less then the width of the flexbox container. These utilities control how the extra spacing is allocated.

Three utilities squeeze the elements together as closely as possible:

- justify-start places the elements against the beginning of the axis, based on the text direction.

- justify-end puts the items against the end of the axis.

- justify-center centers the items—a longstanding CSS frustration.

Three utilities space the elements, and they differ in exactly where the spacing is placed:

- justify-between places the first element against the beginning of the flexbox, the last element against the end of the flexbox, and then even spacing between internal elements. If the flexbox has three items, you get two identically sized spaces with a pattern of AxBxC.

- justify-evenly places an equal amount of space around each item. If the flexbox has three items, four identically sized spaces are placed around them with a pattern of xAxBxCx.

- justify-around places identical spacing around each side of each item. In practice, this makes the end spacing less than the internal space because each internal space contains the left space of one element and the right space of the other. If the flexbox has three items, six equally sized spaces are placed around them with a pattern of xAxxBxxCx.

An element's placing within its individual box can be controlled with a class on the container, with the options being justify-items-start, justify-items-end, and justify-items-center for placement. If you want the item to expand to fill its space, you've got justify-items-stretch, and the reset option is justify-items-auto. Note that you'd normally use either a regular justify- to space items or a justify-items- to space items within its box, but you wouldn't normally need to do both. If a single element of the box wants to override the container's justification, you can use justify-self-{option} with the same five options that exist for justify-items.

Cross Axis

The utilities along the cross axis are all analogous to those of the main axis. Instead of justify-, Tailwind offers content- with the same six options, so content-start pushes items against the top of a multi-row flexbox, while content-center vertically centers them.

For an individual item, you have the same five options as for justify-items-, but the prefix is simply items-. So items-center vertically centers items along the cross axis. Similarly, the same five options exist for a self override, but the prefix is only self-, as in self-start or self-center.

Finally, you can manage both axes at the same time with the prefixes place-content-, place-items-, and place-self-, with the result equivalent to having done both the main and cross axis spacing. So place-content-center is equivalent to the combined justify-center and content-center, while place-items-start is equivalent to justify-items-start and items-start.

Now, let's see how we can make these Tailwind utilities provide more dynamic behavior.

CHAPTER 6

Animation

In this chapter, we're going to look at animations and transitions, which allow you to move items around the page using CSS properties. Tailwind doesn't provide a full implementation of CSS animation and transformation behavior—that'd be a lot to ask of a utility framework. It does provide useful defaults for common behaviors, but even the Tailwind documentation admits that these are only suggestions and that most projects that use animation will need to define custom behavior.

Helpful Small Animations

Tailwind provides four full animation utilities: animate-bounce, animate-ping, animate-pulse, and animate-spin. These classes define both the CSS for an animation and a set of keyframes, so you can use them on an element as is.

The first utility, animate-bounce, describes a one-second transition translating the vertical position down by 25% of the size of the element and then back to the original position, so it gives a slight downward bounce. For example, you could use hover:animate-bounce to give a nice "you are here" effect.

You can give a notification effect a little animation with the second utility, animate-ping, which is a one-second animation from regular size and opacity to twice the size and 0 opacity, which gives a pretty effective signal pulse effect.

A common load behavior is to have dummy elements display and be gradually replaced by data as the server provides it. The third Tailwind utility, animate-pulse, gives you a two-second transition between 0.1 opacity and 0.5, which produces a slight fade effect on the element.

The final utility, animate-spin, animates a full rotation of an object 360 degrees in one second. It's designed to be used for things like a loading status marker.

If you have an SVG or image you want to use, add animate-spin to the SVG or image element (not its container), and the element will rotate.

All of these are negated by animate-none.

Transitions

In CSS, you can specify that one or more properties should gradually transition when they change values, rather than changing instantly. In a full client-side application, you might change values by using JavaScript to modify the CSS classes on an element. In Tailwind, you can use the modifiers to manage some CSS property changes merely in CSS. For example, an element with a class list of "bg-green-500 hover:bg-yellow-500" will change color from green to yellow when the user hovers over it, and the Tailwind transition utilities can make that happen gradually.

In most cases, you'd declare an element to have a class of transition, which causes the element to use transition effects for the CSS properties, background-color, border-color, box-shadow, color, fill, opacity, stroke, and transform. Often that's all the properties you want to transition, but if you need to transition other properties, you can use transition-all to place all properties under the transition banner.

If you want to limit the transition to certain properties, Tailwind provides several choices. Typically you would use these because there are changes in other properties that you want to happen instantly.

transition-color

transition-opacity

transition-shadow

transition-transform

For the transition to actually be visible, you need to specify a duration over which the transition will take place. The default is 0 (but can be changed in the Tailwind configuration), and Tailwind provides the duration-{milliseconds} family of utilities, where the suffix is one of 75, 100, 150, 200, 300, 500, 700, or 1000, indicating the number of milliseconds the transition should cover, and allowing for the arbitrary value syntax.

You can also delay the start of the transition with delay-{milliseconds} and the same set of numbers or arbitrary values, indicating the number of milliseconds before the transition should start.

By default, the transition is applied linearly, meaning the change to the property happens in a series of identically sized steps. That default is denoted by the Tailwind utility, ease-linear. If you want the property change to start more slowly, speed up, and then slow down as it gets closer to the end, you can use ease-in-out. (Or you can use either ease-in or ease-out if you only want the slowdown on one side of the change.) The ease difference is subtle, but especially with motion, it can provide a sense of a change accelerating and then decelerating in a way that can look more natural and engaging.

Transformation

CSS allows you to transform the box of an element in various ways, changing its size, location, rotation, or skew. Tailwind again gives you some reasonable defaults, which when combined with transitions and animation can allow you to build some great effects easily.

Changing the Scale

Tailwind lets you change the scale of an element with the scale-{percentage} family, where the suffix is the percentage to scale. The default, nonarbitrary, options are 0, 50, 75, 90, 95, 100, 105, 110, 125, and 150, which are, I think, designed to allow for subtle effects like "transition duration-1000 hover:scale-110" (which would make an element get slightly bigger on hover over the course of a second). Add in hover:box-shadow-lg, and it'd seem like the element was getting closer to the user on hover.

If you only want to scale in one direction, you can use scale-x-{percentage} or scale-y-{percentage} with the same set of numbers (scale-x-95, scale-y-125, and so on).

Rotating

You can rotate an element with rotate-{degrees}, which is a clockwise transformation of a number of degrees. The provided options are 0, 1, 2, 3, 6, 12, 45, 90, and 180, and arbitrary values can use different units. A counterclockwise rotation is achieved with -rotate-{degrees} and the same numbers.

Again, the design here is to make it easy for small effects. The rotation is, by default, around an axis in the middle of the element, which Tailwind denotes as origin-center. You can move the origin around by adding the suffixes for the same four directions and four corners that you've seen elsewhere to origin- (for example, origin-top, origin-bottom-right, and so on).

Skew and Translate

For skew, you have skew-x-{degrees}, -skew-x-{degrees}, skew-y-{degrees}, and -skew-y-{degrees}, which take as provided options the numerical suffixes 0, 1, 2, 3, 6, or 12, as the number of degrees in the skew.

You can flat out move an element with translate-x-{size}, -translate-x-{size}, translate-y-{size}, or -translate-y-{size}, each of which takes a numerical suffix. This moves the element along the direction using the same number scale you've seen for padding, margins, and the like, where each number represents 0.25rem. Positive directions are right and down, and negative directions are left and up.

In addition to the number set, you have as suffixes px for a single pixel, full for "move this the exact amount of its size in that dimension," and 1/2 for "move it half the amount of its size in that dimension," as in translate-x-full or translate-y-1/2.

Other Appearance Things

You can also do other changes to cursors and text. You can override the cursor the user sees on hover with another standard cursor by using the utilities cursor-auto, cursor-default, cursor-move, cursor-not-allowed, cursor-pointer, cursor-text, and cursor-wait.

You can disallow text selection for copy and paste purposes in an element with select-none and allow it with select-text, or make the entire text autoselect on click with select-all. (Please don't do this. It's somewhat user-hostile, but you may be asked to for certain kinds of perceived security or compliance reasons.)

You can also give an element a resize handle with resize, and limit the handle to one direction with resize-x or resize-y, and reset it with reset-none.

Next, let's look at how Tailwind allows us to make our site look great at different screen sizes.

CHAPTER 7

Responsive Design

All the examples we've seen so far in this book have one thing in common: they're designed for computer screens and aren't designed to look good on smaller screens, like on a smartphone or tablet. The process of making a CSS design that works on multiple-sized screens is called *responsive design*.

In plain CSS, responsive design can be a complicated tangle of CSS classes and @media tags. Tailwind provides modifiers that can be applied to any Tailwind utility to control the set of screen sizes.

Tailwind doesn't take away all the complexity of responsive design; you still need to consider many factors when you're designing for multiple sizes. For example, you need to think about which elements of your site are most important and need to be emphasized when the user is looking at a smaller screen. But Tailwind does make it easier to experiment with different designs at different sizes and to be able to see all the different size behaviors at a glance. That said, responsive design in Tailwind can lead to extremely long CSS class declarations that can be hard to read.

In this chapter, we'll take a look at the responsive utilities in Tailwind as well as common patterns for applying them.

Tailwind Screen Widths and Breakpoints

In CSS, various properties may be applied conditionally based on the width of the screen. These conditions are managed with the @media tag. The specific screen widths at which the design changes are often called *breakpoints*. In Tailwind, you can put a responsive modifier on any Tailwind utility to specify the minimum screen width where that utility should be applied.

Tailwind's responsive behavior is a little different than you might be used to from other frameworks. Some important behaviors to note include:

- Any responsive modifier causes the utility to take effect at the specified screen width or any larger screen width.

- Tailwind utilities define a minimum width to take effect but not a maximum width.

- If no modifier is used, the default minimum width is 0—the utility is always in effect.

If you define something as being for small screen widths, Tailwind applies that behavior all the way up—small, medium, large, and beyond. If you want behavior only on small screens, you define the small-screen behavior without a modifier and the canceling behavior with a mid-screen or wide-screen modifier.

Tailwind defines five screen widths by default. For these five screen widths, the pixel width is the logical width of the screen. On a device with a retina screen, where a logical pixel would be made up of more than one physical pixel, we still use the logical screen. The iPhone 13 is 390 logical pixels wide, for example, even though it is 1170 physical pixels wide.

The five screen widths are:

Small (sm:)—640 pixels and up

Medium (md:)—768 pixels and up

Large (lg:)—1024 pixels and up

Extra large (xl:)—1280 pixels and up

Extra extra large (2xl:)—1536 pixels and up

The following table offers a partial list of existing device widths:[1]

Device	Logical Pixels
Galaxy S20	360
Galaxy S20 sideways	800
iPhone 13	390
iPhone 13 sideways	844
iPad Air 3	834
iPad Air 3 sideways	1112
iPad Pro 12"	1024
iPad Pro 12" sideways	1366
MacBook Air	2560 (often scaled to 1680)

1.   https://ios-resolution.com

The key point is that if you define something as sm: (for example, sm:m-2), that m-2 utility is defined for all screens that are sized 640 pixels and up. If you want to change that margin on a larger screen, you can define a utility with a larger modifier—you are guaranteed that the larger modifiers will take priority over smaller ones. So you could do sm:m-2 md:m-4 lg:m-8 to have your margin get progressively wider as you have more screen width.

The general way to approach these patterns is this: the utilities that don't have modifiers should describe the behavior you see on the smallest screen, and then you bring in modified utilities to adjust behavior as the screen gets bigger. The idea is that you'll define your design for mobile devices first and then use the modifiers to adjust the design for larger screens.

I've tried to be consistent throughout the book about pointing out negation or default utilities even when it isn't clear where they might be used. The responsive utilities are where these negation utilities are used. In Tailwind, the width modifiers apply at their size and up. If you want to unapply a utility at a wider width, you need to negate it explicitly at the larger width. For example, something like sm:shadow-xl md:shadow-none uses the .shadow-none reset utility to undo the .shadow-xl. Using both of these on an element would give you a box shadow for a width between 640 and 768 (if for some reason you wanted to do that).

It's worth mentioning that you can combine screen size with other modifiers: md:hover:font-bold lg:hover:font-black is perfectly legal.

Hide Based on Size

One way to make your application fit on a smaller screen is by hiding parts of the user interface on the smaller screen. In this case, because the smallest screen behavior is hidden, the unmodified property is hidden. At larger sizes, you might want the item to display, so you add in lg:block (or whatever breakpoint you want to start seeing the item at), winding up with class="hidden lg:block".

Sometimes you may want to go the other way and display an element at a smaller size but not at a larger one. It's quite common to have an element for a hamburger menu replace a navigation bar on small size, but then disappear on a device that's large enough to show all the navigation. In that case, the small-size behavior is to display, which is the default, and you add the hiding behavior in as a breakpoint, as in class="lg:hidden".

Similarly, it's common to drop the size of header text on smaller devices. The smaller size is what displays on the smaller widths, so the resulting DOM classes would look something like class="text-xl md:text-2xl lg:text-4xl". (See Duplication, on page 12, for hints on how to avoid needing to constantly type all that.)

Fewer Grid Columns on Small Devices

In general terms, the goal of a lot of responsive design is to simultaneously allow information to be stacked at small sizes and spread out into rows when the space exists at larger sizes. Exactly how you want to do this depends on your goal.

One possibility is that you have a set of card-like elements, something like the featured posts on a news site, where the data isn't actually a table but a series of items laid out in a row.

In this case, you might want the items to fill the entire width of the screen but the number of items to vary based on the size of the screen. On a smartphone, you might want only one item across the screen; on a desktop, maybe four. So you can use something like this:

```
<div class="grid items-stretch
            md:grid-cols-2 md:gap-4
            lg:grid-cols-4 lg:gap-4">
  <div class="mb-6 lg:mb-0"></div>
  ...
</div>
```

A couple of things are going on here. The parent div is a grid at all widths, but the default grid size at the narrowest width is 1, growing to 2 on a medium screen and to 4 on a large screen. items-stretch means that each individual child element will stretch to fill its portion of the width, which means they'll get bigger as the screen gets bigger until the next breakpoint and then more items will be added to each row. We also increase the gap between items as the screen gets bigger. For the child items, we have margin bottom mb-6 when only one element is in the row so that there's some spacing, but the margin bottom goes away when the screen gets larger, with lg:mb-0.

Flex on Larger Devices

Another way to adjust between sizes is to have an element use default block spacing on smaller devices and then convert to flex spacing on larger devices. The block spacing on small devices ensures that the items stay in a column, even if some of them are narrow, while the flex spacing at a larger size spreads them out in a row.

The common pattern here is a navigation bar that's spread over the top of the page at a larger size. But at a smaller size, it's a menu column, generally hidden until the menu button is clicked.

Here's a simple example:

```
<div class="w-full hidden lg:flex lg:flex-grow, lg:items-center lg:width-auto
    divide-black divide-y lg:divide-y-0"
    id="navbar-menu">
  <a class="block lg:mr-4 p-2 hover:bg-gray-200">Blog</a>
  ...
</div>
```

The outer div here is hidden on small screens to start. This is usually paired with JavaScript (which we'll do in a second) to make it not hidden. On a small screen, when it's unhidden it'll use the default display mode of block, meaning columns. At larger sizes, the lg:flex overrides the hidden utility, and the display is flex and flex-grow, meaning the items will fit across the screen. I've also added a dividing line between items at small scale, divide-y, but the line goes away at larger sizes. lg:divide-y-0 makes the items more distinguishable in the small column.

The inner items have a little bit more right margin at large sizes, and they change their background to gray on hover. They need to be explicitly set to block because a tags are inline by default. If I'd made those div tabs, the block wouldn't be needed.

To make this work as a navbar, you need a little JavaScript. The following snippet, which is vanilla JavaScript without a framework, assumes you have three elements. One is the navbar itself, which we previously discussed, but with a DOM ID of navbar-menu. The other two elements are hidden in the same spacing and are the hamburger menu, navbar-burger, and an x-shaped close element, navbar-close:

```
<nav class="flex items-center font-bold text-grey=600">
  <div class="block lg:hidden self-start">
    <button id="navbar-burger"
            class="px-3 py-2
                   border rounded border-grey-400
                   hover:border-black">
      <svg xmlns="http://www.w3.org/2000/svg"
           fill="none" viewBox="0 0 24 24"
           stroke="currentColor">
        <path stroke-linecap="round"
              stroke-linejoin="round"
              stroke-width="2"
              d="M4 6h16M4 12h16M4 18h16" />
      </svg>
    </button>
    <button id="navbar-close"
            class="px-3 py-2
                   border rounded border-grey-400
                   hover:border-black">
```

```
        <svg xmlns="http://www.w3.org/2000/svg"
             fill="none"
             viewBox="0 0 24 24"
             stroke="currentColor">
          <path stroke-linecap="round"
                stroke-linejoin="round"
                stroke-width="2"
                d="M6 18L18 6M6 6l12 12" />
        </svg>
      </button>
    </div>
    <div class="w-full hidden
               lg:flex lg:flex-grow,
               lg:items-center lg:width-auto
               divide-black divide-y
               lg:divide-y-0"
               id="navbar-menu">
      <a class="block lg:mr-4 p-2 hover:bg-gray-200">Blog</a>
      AND SO ON
    </div>
  </div>
</div>
</nav>
```

The SVG for the hamburger and close icons comes from https://heroicons.com, a set of small SVG icons that are also from the makers of Tailwind CSS.

Next, we add an event listener to the navbar burger and navbar close. The burger listener hides the burger and shows the close button and the menu. The close listener hides the close button and menu and shows the burger:

```
document.addEventListener('DOMContentLoaded', () => {
  const $navbarBurger = document.querySelector('#navbar-burger')
  const $navbarClose = document.querySelector('#navbar-close')
  const $navbarMenu = document.querySelector('#navbar-menu')

  $navbarBurger.addEventListener('click', () => {
    $navbarMenu.classList.remove("hidden")
    $navbarBurger.classList.add("hidden")
    $navbarClose.classList.remove("hidden")
  });

  $navbarClose.addEventListener('click', () => {
    $navbarMenu.classList.add("hidden")
    $navbarBurger.classList.remove("hidden")
    $navbarClose.classList.add("hidden")
  });
})
```

And that gives you a basic responsive navigation system. Season to taste.

Next, let's talk about how to customize Tailwind.

CHAPTER 8

Customizing Tailwind

Throughout this book, I've alluded to the idea that Tailwind is customizable, and here's where I explain how and why. Tailwind is an engine that generates many CSS classes based on the patterns in your code, and this engine has a lot of hooks that allow us to alter the set of utilities available to us.

You might want to customize Tailwind for several reasons:

- *Change defaults.* Tailwind provides default step values for most of its utilities, for example, the common steps for margins, padding, and other spacing items. And it has default screen sizes for responsive breakpoints. Tailwind also provides a default set of colors, but you may want to add your own. In the configuration file, you can change these. Even though you can use arbitrary values in the places where you can insert values, commonly used one-offs are easier to manage and shorter to type if you turn them into defaults.

- *Change the set of classes.* Tailwind generates a lot of CSS classes. And even though it produces classes based on your own code, you might still want to explicitly prevent certain classes from being generated or ensure other classes are generated.

- *Add new behavior.* Although you can write your own extensions in regular CSS, you can also add new items as plugins that are part of the Tailwind configuration, which can make them easier to share and to integrate with other Tailwind behavior.

- *Integrate with legacy CSS.* You may want to start using Tailwind on a site that already has a lot of CSS. Tailwind provides configuration options that allow you to ensure that Tailwind utilities don't conflict with existing CSS or with the limitations of your HTML templating tool.

Let's take a look at how to customize Tailwind to your liking, starting with the configuration file.

Configuration File Basics

The configuration file is optionally generated as part of your Tailwind installation. You can also create it at any time after you install the Tailwind npm package with the command, npx tailwindcss init. The minimal configuration file looks like this:

```
module.exports = {
  content: [],
  theme: {
    extend: {},
  },
  plugins: [],
}
```

If for some reason you want a configuration file with the entire default configuration explicitly listed, you can get it with npx tailwindcss init --full. Most of what we're going to be looking at will go in the theme section.

Tailwind considers each family of utilities to be a *core plugin*; you can see a complete list in the Tailwind documentation.[1] The theme object references these core plugin names to allow you to customize the core plugins—most of the core plugins have customization options.

Change Default Values

In the configuration file, the theme object has keys that are the names of each core plugin and values that are the configuration options for that plugin. The three special configuration options, screen, color, and spacing, aren't core plugins themselves but are the basis for the configuration of many other core plugins.

It's worth mentioning here that Tailwind's use of the word "theme" is different than the way you might see it used in other places, where "theme" refers to a set of colors, as in "dark theme" versus "light theme." For Tailwind, the theme is the entire set of defaults, and there's only one. If you want to change color schemes, you need to either use CSS variables or use the dark: modifier to specify behavior under dark mode. (You can see the entire default theme on GitHub.[2] This is the theme in the main branch of Tailwind, so it may be slightly ahead of the released version.)

You can customize the theme in two ways: (1) override entire options or (2) extend options.

---

1.   https://tailwindcss.com/docs/configuration#core-plugins
2.   https://github.com/tailwindlabs/tailwindcss/blob/master/stubs/defaultConfig.stub.js

To override, you provide a new set of values for an entire object—either a core plugin or one of the special values—in the theme object. This example changes the entire set of screen breakpoints. Overriding the theme object this way completely replaces the default values:

```
theme: {
    screens: {
        'phone': '640px',
        'landscape': '768px',
        'tablet': '1024px',
        'laptop': '1280px',
    }
}
```

If you want to preserve the existing default values but add new ones on top, you can use theme#extend. This configuration adds an extra, extra-wide screen breakpoint:

```
theme: {
  extend: {
    screens: {
      3xl: '2440px',
    }
  }
}
```

Screen Widths

The screens object inside the key generates the breakpoints used for the responsive modifiers. The default looks like this:

```
module.exports = {
  theme: {
    screens: {
      'sm': '640px',
      'md': '768px',
      'lg': '1024px',
      'xl': '1280px',
      '2xl': '1536px',
    }
  }
}
```

You can modify this in many ways, but note that if you modify the values here, you need to provide the entire range of sizes. If you only want to add a new size, you need to go to the extend subject of themes:

```
module.exports = {
  theme: {
    screens: {
```

```
      extend: {
        3xl: '2440px',
      }
    }
  }
}
```

These breakpoints are a reasonable set of defaults, but if you only want to move the values around and about, you can do that here.

You can also change the names of the keys to something like phone, landscape, tablet, and desktop. Those keys then become the names of your modifiers, so you'd no longer write sm:m-0; you'd write phone:m-0.

If the value you provide for the screen-width keys is a string, it's considered the min-width of the breakpoint when generating the CSS. You can also pass an object with min and max keys if you want to specify the breakpoints differently. If you only specify max values, then the responsive behavior is reversed. Unmodified utilities apply at the largest size, and modifiers take effect as the screen gets smaller:

```
module.exports = {
  theme: {
    screens: {
      '2xl': {'max': '9999px'},
      'xl': {'max': '1535px'},
      'lg': {'max': '1023px'},
      'md': {'max': '767px'},
      'sm': {'max': '639px'},
    }
  }
}
```

You can also supply a min value to those objects, which limits each breakpoint to a specific range and means that you need to completely specify all properties at each breakpoint.

Media queries aren't only based on size. If you want to base a modifier on something else, you can do so with a raw option. Here's a configuration that adds a print mode:

```
module.exports = {
  theme: {
    extend: {
      screens: { 'print': {'raw': 'print'} },
    }
  }
}
```

You can then use this configuration like any other screen with class="print:bg-white".

Default Colors

Tailwind has a common set of colors that's used as a suffix for many utility families, including text-, bg-, and others. Tailwind provides 22 colors. If you want to change that set, you can reach them via a colors object:

```
module.exports = {
  theme: {
    colors: {
      gray: colors.warmGray,
      red: colors.red,
      green: colors.green,
    }
  }
}
```

The complete list of colors is in the Tailwind documentation.[3]

While you can completely replace the set of colors in theme#colors, you're more likely to want to add your own extra colors in theme#extend#colors, like this:

```
module.exports = {
  theme: {
    extend: {
      colors: {
        "company-orange": "#ff5715",
        "company-dark-blue": "#323C64",
        "company-gray": "#DADADA",
      }
    }
  }
}
```

Now you can use text-company-orange or bg-company-gray. You can also add color families by using the same colors object as the value to any key.

You can also nest the colors to remove duplication:

```
module.exports = {
  theme: {
    extend: {
      colors: {
        "company": {
          "orange": "#ff5715",
```

---

3. https://tailwindcss.com/docs/customizing-colors

```
          "dark-blue": "#323C64",
          "gray": " #DADADA",
        }
      }
    }
  }
}
```

The resulting classes are still the same as the unnested colors were, like text-company-orange, for example. If you only want text-company, then using the key default will stand in for the unsuffixed value.

If you extend colors with an existing color, for example if you provide red: { '100': "#WHATEVER" }, you'll replace the existing red family with your new set.

If you want to extend a color with a new level, you can use the spread operator:

```
module.exports = {
  theme: {
    extend: {
      colors: {
        "red": {
          ...colors.red,
          "450": " #CC0000",
        }
      }
    }
  }
}
```

But What If I Really Want Color Themes?

The closest you can get to color themes in standard Tailwind is by using the dark: modifier. To enable the dark: modifier, you need to add this line to your Tailwind configuration:

```
module.exports = {
  darkMode: "media",
}
```

With that in place, you can now use the modifier dark: to specify behavior that changes when the browser is in dark mode. So, you can have a class list that's something like class="bg-gray-100 dark:bg-gray-900 text-gray-700 dark:text-gray-100".

The dark: modifier can be stacked with other modifiers like hover: and with responsive modifiers like sm:.

If darkMode is set to media, then Tailwind uses the prefers-color-scheme media setting of the browser. If you'd rather control the mode setting yourself, you can set darkMode to class, and then Tailwind adds a utility class dark, which changes any element inside that class to dark mode. Typically, you'd put that at the top of your DOM tree and use JavaScript so you can change the entire tree at once:

```
<body class="container mx-auto py-12 px-6 dark">
  <div class="bg-gray-100 dark:bg-black">
  </div>
</body>
```

You can do more elaborate things with custom themes and CSS variables. You'll find a good overview at dev.to.[4]

Spacing

Spacing, as used for padding, margins, width, height, and other properties, can also be overridden by using theme#spacing or extended with theme#extend#spacing. So you could simply replace the spacing like this:

```
module.exports = {
  theme: {
    spacing: {
      'small': 4px,
      'medium': 12px,
      'large': 36px
    }
  }
}
```

These new suffixes would apply anywhere spacing goes, so you'd now have p-small, h-medium, gap-large, or other possibilities.

If you like the existing scale but want more options, then use the extends option:

```
module.exports = {
  theme: {
    extend: {
      spacing: {
        '15': '60rem',
        '17': '76rem'
      }
    }
  }
}
```

Other Core Plugins

Nearly every Tailwind utility has a series of suffixes off of a base pattern. And nearly all of them allow you to override or extend them the same way you do for spacing and colors.

---

4. https://dev.to/ohitslaurence/creating-dynamic-themes-with-react-tailwindcss-59cl

I'll pick one example, as doing all of them is outside the scope of this book. Every core plugin's page in the Tailwind documentation explains how to modify that plugin. You can add different z-index values in the configuration file with theme#extend:

```
module.exports = {
  theme: {
    extend: {
      zIndex: {
        "-1": "-1",
        "-5": "-5",
        "-1000": "-1000"
      }
    }
  }
}
```

Note that in this case, Tailwind generates the negative classes with a pattern consistent with negative margins, so the negative classes here are -z-1, -z-5, and -z-1000.

If I want my own complete set of z-index options, then I wouldn't use extend:

```
module.exports = {
  theme: {
    zIndex: {
      "1": "1",
      "5": "5",
      "1000": "1000"
      "-1": "-1",
      "-5": "-5",
      "-1000": "-1000"
    }
  }
}
```

Now I have z-1, z-5, and z-100 alongside -z-1, -z-5, and -z-1000, but the original classes are no longer generated.

Every core plugin with multiple options allows for similar replacement or extension of the options. Again, the Tailwind documentation has a full listing.

Change Generated Classes

Under normal circumstances, the Tailwind compiler generates CSS only for the class names that are used in your application. However, under some circumstances you might want to modify that configuration.

First, here's what the compiler does.

The configuration file has a content key that should contain a list of file patterns for any file in your project that might reference a Tailwind utility. This includes your static .html files, but also your .jsx files for a React project or .erb files for a Rails project. It even includes other files that might reference Tailwind utilities that are called by template files. (But don't include other .css files—you want to list the files that use Tailwind classes, not the files that define Tailwind classes.)

The file patterns use the fast-glob library, which includes * to match any text except a directory marker, ** to match any text including directory markers (allowing you to match arbitrary subdirectories), and curly braces and commas to allow for options, as in *.{html, erb}.

If you use the strategies described in Duplication, on page 12, to define lists of Tailwind classes in JavaScript or Ruby or whatever, those files also need to be listed in the content field of the configuration file. You might wind up with something like this for a React project:

```
module.exports = {
  content: [
    "./src/**/*.{html, jsx, tsx}",
  ],
}
```

A Rails project might look like this:

```
module.exports = {
  content: [
    "./app/views/**/*.{html, erb}",
    "./app/helpers/**/*.rb"
  ],
}
```

You want to be a little careful here. Classes that are used in files that are not in the content list will not generate CSS and will appear to not work. (In a Rails context, this has bitten me where CSS classes were defined in a one-off initializer in config/initializers.)

On the other hand, while the cost of including non-front-end files is small, the cost of including, say, your entire node-modules directory is high, both in the time it takes to run the command-line tool and in the amount of unneeded CSS it would generate.

The mechanism Tailwind uses is simple by design. It tries to split the associated files into individual words and then matches it against a list of Tailwind patterns to determine which words are potential Tailwind utilities that need CSS to be generated for them.

This process errs on the side of caution in that it might capture class names not being used as class names, which is generally fine and a million times easier than trying to guess in the general case what is a real CSS class and what is just a line of JavaScript or a comment.

What it won't catch is a class name that's dynamically created via string concatenation.

In Chapter 3, Typography, on page 19, we looked at the following example for creating a hover effect:

```
const hoverDarker = (color) => {
  return `text-${color}-300 hover:text-${color}-700`
}
```

This function, because it creates a class name dynamically, would prevent those classes from being found by Tailwind, so you'd either need to use those classes elsewhere or find another way to create this feature.

One option would be a safelist. Tailwind provides a configuration key called safelist that allows you to specify Tailwind classes that you want to guarantee will be generated. The individual listings in the safelist can be strings or JavaScript regular expressions, with some limitations:

```
module.exports = {
  content: [
    "./app/views/**/*.{html, erb}",
    "./app/helpers/**/*.rb"
  ],
  safelist: [
    "bg-red-300",
    "bg-red-700",
    {
      pattern: /bg-(gray|slate|zinc|neutral|stone)-(300|700)/,
      variants: ["hover"]
    }
  ]
}
```

This configuration file safelists two background colors individually, then matches all the grayscale ones with the regular expression. The pattern of the regular expression must start with a Tailwind utility. For example, you couldn't match all the places gray is used with +.-gray-+., but you can match all red background colors and opacities with bg-red-+.\\+.. I also don't think you could match, say, box and border with bo+.. (At the very least, it's probably a bad idea.) You can't match modifiers in the safelist pattern, but you can make sure the modifiers are generated by including the modifiers you want generated in the list of variants as part of the configuration.

You can also create a block list of core plugins by passing an object to the corePlugins key of the configuration. The keys of this object are the name of core plugins you want to eliminate, and the values are all false. You'd only do this if you wanted to block classes you are actually using for some reason:

```
module.exports = {
  corePlugins: {
    flex: false,
    flexDirection: false,
    flexGrow: false,
    flexShrink: false,
    flexWrap: false,
  }
}
```

This configuration gets rid of all the flexbox-related tools, though I don't recommend doing that. Flexbox is pretty useful.

Variant Modifiers

We've seen variant modifiers in Tailwind like hover and focus, but Tailwind defines a couple dozen modifiers, and the command-line tool only generates the CSS for modifier combinations you actually use.

In addition to the screen size modifiers sm, md, lg, xl, and 2xl, following is a partial tour of the Tailwind modifiers:

- active: Applies when the element is active.

- dark: Applies if Tailwind thinks it's in dark mode.

- first-letter: Applies to the first letter of the text.

- first-line: Applies to the first line of the text.

- hover: Applies when the user is hovering the pointer over the element.

- landscape: Applies if the device is in landscape orientation.

- ltr: Applies for text going left to right.

- marker: Applies to the list marker.

- motion-reduce: Applies if the user has enabled reduce motion on the system. It's often applied with hover, and you'd often have a motion-reduce and a motion-safe variant.

- motion-safe: Applies if the user has *not* enabled reduce motion on the system. It's often applied with hover, and you'd often have a motion-reduce and a motion-safe variant.

- portrait: Applies if the device is in portrait orientation.

- print: Applies for the print media type.

- rtl: Applies for text going right to left.

- selection: Applies to text selected by the user.

- target: Applies if the element ID matches the current URL.

- visited: Applies if a link has been visited.

Two group properties work by declaring a parent element with the class group. These variant properties apply when any element in the parent is targeted, not only the element in question:

- group-focus: Applies to any child when any child under the parent gets the focus.

- group-hover: Applies to any child when the parent is hovered over. It's enabled by default wherever hover is enabled.

A few properties are applied based on the order of the elements within their parent. These variants would go on the child element, not the parent element, and are particularly helpful if your template language is generating an entire loop:

- empty: Applies if the element has no children.

- even: Applies if the element is an even-number child (second, fourth, sixth, and so on).

- first: Applies if the element is the first (topmost) child of its parent element. Also, first-of-type.

- last: Applies if the element is the last (bottommost) child of its parent element. Also, last-of-type.

- odd: Applies if the element is an odd-numbered child (first, third, fifth, and so on).

- only: Applies if the element is an only child, also only-of-type.

A few properties apply to form elements:

- autofill: Applies if the box has been autofilled by the browser.

- checked: Applies if the checkbox or radio button has been checked.

- default: Applies if the element still has its default value.

- disabled: Applies when the element is disabled.

- file: Applies to the button in a file input.

- focus: Applies when the element has focus, as in a text field.

- focus-within: Applies to a parent class when any child inside that parent has focus.

- indeterminate: Applies if a checkbox or radio button is in the indeterminate state.

- in-range: Applies if the element's value is in range, as in a number spinner.

- invalid: Applies if the element has an invalid value.

- out-of-range: Applies if the element's value is out of range, as in a number spinner.

- placeholder: Applies to placeholder text.

- placeholder-shown: Applies if the placeholder text is still being shown.

- read-only: Applies if the element is read-only.

- required: Applies if the element is required.

Tailwind also uses before and after to match the ::before and ::after pseudo-classes.

Integrate with Existing CSS

One problem you might have if you're using Tailwind in conjunction with a lot of existing CSS is name conflict. Your existing CSS might already define hidden, flex-grow, or (admittedly less likely) mx-64. Tailwind gives you a way to prevent this problem by offering you the ability to put a common prefix in front of all Tailwind utilities: prefix: "<SOMETHING>". If you declare prefix: "twind", then all the Tailwind utilities are transformed, so you end up with twind-hidden, twind-flex-grow, and even twind-mx-64. If you have a modifier, it attaches normally, as in hover:twind-text-black.

A different problem is that your existing CSS may be set up in such a way that all the existing CSS selectors have high specificity and thus override all of the Tailwind utilities. You can get around this with a configuration of important: true, which adds the CSS marker !important to all the Tailwind utilities, which should give them precedence over existing CSS. This can have unwanted side effects if you're using a lot of different CSS libraries, so be careful with it.

Some template tools don't allow you to use the colon (:) character in class names, making Tailwind's prefixes illegal. You can specify a separator: option to choose your own separator, so separator: "--" means prefixes would look like hover--text-black or lg--m0-4. (I think I like the look of that more than the colon.)

Access Tailwind from JavaScript

You can access Tailwind configuration from JavaScript. This is useful if you want to use those values to create dynamic behavior in your JavaScript framework. You might have some kind of custom animation that needs to respect existing colors or spacing, or who knows what.

Whatever you want to do, Tailwind provides a resolveConfig method that takes as an argument the Tailwind configuration object and allows you to query the configuration—the full configuration, not only your overrides in the file:

```
import resolveConfig from 'tailwindcss/resolveConfig'
import myConfig from './tailwind.config.js'

const tailwindConfig = resolveConfig(myConfig)

tailwindConfig.theme.colors
```

The resulting object from resolveConfig merges your configuration overrides with the defaults and provides an object you can query.

Plugins

Tailwind plugins are just snippets of JavaScript that you can define that allow you to insert your own additional classes, patterns, and prefixes to your Tailwind app. They are actually simple enough that you can insert them inline in your Tailwind configuration file.

To start, you need to require the plugin function by putting this line at the top of your tailwind.config.js file:

```
const plugin = require("taiwindcss/plugin")
```

Then, inside the configuration itself, you can call that plugin function. The argument to plugin is a function.

```
const plugin = require("taiwindcss/plugin")

module.exports = {
  content: ["./html/*.html"],
```

```
  theme: {
    extend: {},
  },
  plugins: [
    plugin(({}) => {
    })
  ],
};
```

The anonymous function takes one argument, which the previous snippet has as an empty JavaScript object, {}. The object that is actually passed to that function has a number of parameters, each of which is a helper function that you can call in the body of the anonymous function to add Tailwind features. Typically, you'd use JavaScript destructuring syntax to only capture the helper functions you want to use.

For example, if you want to add your own variant prefix, one of the helper functions is addVariant(), and you'd use it like this (this adds some extra ordinals):

```
const plugin = require("taiwindcss/plugin")

module.exports = {
  content: ["./html/*.html"],
  theme: {
    extend: {},
  },
  plugins: [
    plugin(({ addVariant }) => {
      addVariant("second-of-type", "&:nth-of-type(2)")
      addVariant("third-of-type", "&:nth-of-type(3)")
    })
  ],
};
```

The addVariant method takes two arguments: (1) the modifier you want to add, and (2) the CSS pseudo-class or media type it should convert to.

Similarly, Tailwind provides helper methods for addUtilities, addComponents, and addBase. The addUtilities method takes two arguments: (1) the name of a new Tailwind utility you want to add, and (2) a JavaScript object with the CSS property you want that utility to resolve to, as in addUtilities(".big-bold-text", {font-size: "1.5rem", font-weight: "700"}). The addComponents helper does the same thing but puts the styles in the Tailwind components layer. The addBase helper adds new styles to the Tailwind base layer, meaning that the first argument is an HTML selector like h4 rather than a CSS class.

There are also matchUtilities and matchComponents methods that allow you to define a set of dynamic matchers. Both of these can use a helper method theme to look up values in the current theme as a way of determining what's in the set of dynamic matchers. So, theme("spacing") gives you all the spacing options. See https://tailwindcss.com/docs/plugins for full documentation.

The End

And with that, we've reached the end of our Tailwind journey. Tailwind changes frequently, so you should check out the Tailwind blog at https://blog.tailwindcss.com for up-to-date changes. Also, you can find a lot of great screencasts, sample components, and other resources linked in the Tailwind documentation at https://tailwindcss.com.

Now, go design something great!

Thank you!

We hope you enjoyed this book and that you're already thinking about what you want to learn next. To help make that decision easier, we're offering you this gift.

Head on over to https://pragprog.com right now, and use the coupon code BUYANOTHER2022 to save 30% on your next ebook. Offer is void where prohibited or restricted. This offer does not apply to any edition of the *The Pragmatic Programmer* ebook.

And if you'd like to share your own expertise with the world, why not propose a writing idea to us? After all, many of our best authors started off as our readers, just like you. With a 50% royalty, world-class editorial services, and a name you trust, there's nothing to lose. Visit https://pragprog.com/become-an-author/ today to learn more and to get started.

We thank you for your continued support, and we hope to hear from you again soon!

The Pragmatic Bookshelf

SAVE 30%!
Use coupon code
BUYANOTHER2022

Rails 5 Test Prescriptions

Does your Rails code suffer from bloat, brittleness, or inaccuracy? Cure these problems with the regular application of test-driven development. You'll use Rails 5.2, Minitest 5, and RSpec 3.7, as well as popular testing libraries such as factory_bot and Cucumber. Updates include Rails 5.2 system tests and Webpack integration. Do what the doctor ordered to make your applications feel all better. Side effects may include better code, fewer bugs, and happier developers.

Noel Rappin
(404 pages) ISBN: 9781680502503. $47.95
https://pragprog.com/book/nrtest3

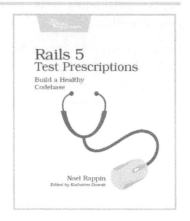

Release It! Second Edition

A single dramatic software failure can cost a company millions of dollars—but can be avoided with simple changes to design and architecture. This new edition of the best-selling industry standard shows you how to create systems that run longer, with fewer failures, and recover better when bad things happen. New coverage includes DevOps, microservices, and cloud-native architecture. Stability antipatterns have grown to include systemic problems in large-scale systems. This is a must-have pragmatic guide to engineering for production systems.

Michael Nygard
(376 pages) ISBN: 9781680502398. $47.95
https://pragprog.com/book/mnee2

Python Testing with pytest, Second Edition

Test applications, packages, and libraries large and small with pytest, Python's most powerful testing framework. pytest helps you write tests quickly and keep them readable and maintainable. In this fully revised edition, explore pytest's superpowers—simple asserts, fixtures, parametrization, markers, and plugins—while creating simple tests and test suites against a small database application. Using a robust yet simple fixture model, it's just as easy to write small tests with pytest as it is to scale up to complex functional testing. This book shows you how.

Brian Okken
(272 pages) ISBN: 9781680508604. $45.95
https://pragprog.com/book/bopytest2

Rails, Angular, Postgres, and Bootstrap, Second Edition

Achieve awesome user experiences and performance with simple, maintainable code! Embrace the full stack of web development, from styling with Bootstrap, building an interactive user interface with Angular 4, to storing data quickly and reliably in PostgreSQL. With this fully revised new edition, take a holistic view of full-stack development to create usable, high-performing applications with Rails 5.1.

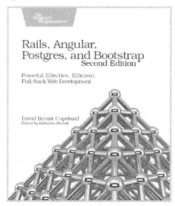

David Bryant Copeland
(342 pages) ISBN: 9781680502206. $39.95
https://pragprog.com/book/dcbang2

Agile Web Development with Rails 6

Learn Rails the way the Rails core team recommends it, along with the tens of thousands of developers who have used this broad, far-reaching tutorial and reference. If you're new to Rails, you'll get step-by-step guidance. If you're an experienced developer, get the comprehensive, insider information you need for the latest version of Ruby on Rails. The new edition of this award-winning classic is completely updated for Rails 6 and Ruby 2.6, with information on processing email with Action Mailbox and managing rich text with Action Text.

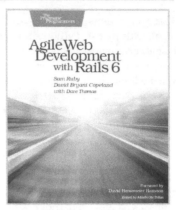

Sam Ruby and David Bryant Copeland
(494 pages) ISBN: 9781680506709. $57.95
https://pragprog.com/book/rails6

The Cucumber Book, Second Edition

Your customers want rock-solid, bug-free software that does exactly what they expect it to do. Yet they can't always articulate their ideas clearly enough for you to turn them into code. You need Cucumber: a testing, communication, and requirements tool—all rolled into one. All the code in this book is updated for Cucumber 2.4, Rails 5, and RSpec 3.5.

Matt Wynne and Aslak Hellesøy, with Steve Tooke
(334 pages) ISBN: 9781680502381. $39.95
https://pragprog.com/book/hwcuc2

Crafting Rails 4 Applications

Get ready to see Rails as you've never seen it before.
Learn how to extend the framework, change its behavior, and replace whole components to bend it to your
will. Eight different test-driven tutorials will help you
understand Rails' inner workings and prepare you to
tackle complicated projects with solutions that are
well-tested, modular, and easy to maintain.

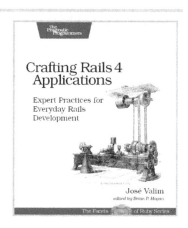

This second edition of the bestselling *Crafting Rails
Applications* has been updated to Rails 4 and discusses
new topics such as streaming, mountable engines, and
thread safety.

José Valim
(208 pages) ISBN: 9781937785550. $36
https://pragprog.com/book/jvrails2

Metaprogramming Ruby 2

Write powerful Ruby code that is easy to maintain and
change. With metaprogramming, you can produce elegant, clean, and beautiful programs. Once the domain
of expert Rubyists, metaprogramming is now accessible
to programmers of all levels. This thoroughly revised
and updated second edition of the bestselling
Metaprogramming Ruby explains metaprogramming in
a down-to-earth style and arms you with a practical
toolbox that will help you write your best Ruby code
ever.

Paolo Perrotta
(276 pages) ISBN: 9781941222126. $38
https://pragprog.com/book/ppmetr2

The Pragmatic Bookshelf

The Pragmatic Bookshelf features books written by professional developers for professional developers. The titles continue the well-known Pragmatic Programmer style and continue to garner awards and rave reviews. As development gets more and more difficult, the Pragmatic Programmers will be there with more titles and products to help you stay on top of your game.

Visit Us Online

This Book's Home Page
https://pragprog.com/book/tailwind2
Source code from this book, errata, and other resources. Come give us feedback, too!

Keep Up to Date
https://pragprog.com
Join our announcement mailing list (low volume) or follow us on twitter @pragprog for new titles, sales, coupons, hot tips, and more.

New and Noteworthy
https://pragprog.com/news
Check out the latest pragmatic developments, new titles and other offerings.

Save on the ebook

Save on the ebook versions of this title. Owning the paper version of this book entitles you to purchase the electronic versions at a terrific discount.

PDFs are great for carrying around on your laptop—they are hyperlinked, have color, and are fully searchable. Most titles are also available for the iPhone and iPod touch, Amazon Kindle, and other popular e-book readers.

Send a copy of your receipt to support@pragprog.com and we'll provide you with a discount coupon.

Contact Us

Online Orders:	*https://pragprog.com/catalog*
Customer Service:	*support@pragprog.com*
International Rights:	*translations@pragprog.com*
Academic Use:	*academic@pragprog.com*
Write for Us:	*http://write-for-us.pragprog.com*
Or Call:	+1 800-699-7764

Lightning Source UK Ltd.
Milton Keynes UK
UKHW031127150622
404468UK00004B/10